'Jesus is the faithful witness, the first among those raised from the dead. He is the ruler of the kings of the earth.' (Rev. 1:5, NCV)

Astounding! Without a doubt, *Ruler of Kings* gets my vote for the most necessary book for the Church today. Not only are there very few books written on the Lordship of Christ in the civil, ethical, and political realm—I can think of none that expound upon it so thoroughly and with such vision. Every few pages I couldn't help shouting to my wife, "This is the book we've been waiting for!"

John Cooper, American musician, singer, songwriter and Co-founder, lead vocalist and bassist of Christian band, Skillet

History teaches us that enduring works of Christian insight flow forth from times of persecution and attack. As secularism rushes toward its inevitable totalitarian solutions, Christians need to think deeply concerning the issues that now confront us. *Ruler of Kings* reminds us that Christ's sceptre of power rules over all of life, and that he will inevitably receive the inheritance of nations. A must read in our day!

James R. White, apologist, theologian and author, and Director of Alpha and Omega Ministries in Phoenix, Arizona

RULER OF KINGS

Toward a Christian Vision of Government

RULER OF KINGS

Toward a Christian Vision of Government

Joseph Boot

Wilberforce Publications
London

Published in Great Britain in 2022 by
Wilberforce Publications Limited
70 Wimpole Street, London W1G 8AX

in association with
Ezra Institute for Contemporary Christianity

*Portions of this book are excerpted from other works, also by Joe Boot,
published by Ezra Press and the Ezra Institute for Contemporary
Christianity:*

- *For Government: Towards a Christian View of Authority (2020)*
- *For Politics: The Christian, the Church and the State (2021)*
- *For the Kingdom of God: A Scriptural Response to a Utopian Social
  Vision (2021)*

Wilberforce Publications Limited is a wholly owned subsidary of
Christian Concern.

ISBN 978-1-9161211-3-3

Printed in Canada by Premier Printing, Winnipeg, Manitoba,
and worldwide by Kindle Direct Publishing

DEDICATION

To John Hultink,
Friend, benefactor, mentor and above all
a good and faithful servant of the King.

CONTENTS

FOREWORD

"Christ not man is King" – so say Oliver Cromwell and Joseph Boot. Jesus is the Ruler of Kings.

Joe Boot gets it, and he serves us a truly Christian Vision of Government.

This book is not for the faint-hearted. Fast-paced, dense (because every word matters), it is a critique of the time we are living in – yes, Joe describes the world as it is today, how it has been changed by growing statism, Covid measures, the cult of the expert and how it is now emerging.

This book is contextual and highly current but its solutions are biblical and therefore enduring. Joe not only understands the times we live in, but he directly, cogently, and provocatively sets out a model for what we should do next.

As someone who has been seeking to contend for Christ as King at the heart of public life in the United Kingdom for the past thirty years, I say that this book is a 'must read' and that you can't read it soon enough. It will make many of us feel uncomfortable as we wrestle with the current reality of the Church's submission in the West to the cult of the State; our surrender to unprecedented lockdowns and illegal interference in church gathering, the collapse of civil liberties, the total control of education, expanded abortion, euthanasia, no-fault divorce law, the redefinition of marriage and family, homosexuality, and transgender issues.

However, the 'culture war' we find ourselves in is not just about these things; for they are only, really, a symptom of the greater cosmic struggle between the Christian worldview and the globalist, utopian view that got us into the world of confusion and control that we now inhabit.

Using rigorous theological, philosophical, and historical analysis, this book challenges to the core traditional Western church leaders' assumptions and responses to Christian participation in cultural, socio-economic and political life.

In its place Joe sets forth a clearly articulated and scripturally grounded Christian political vision that avoids the error of thinking it is all about Christian coercion and domination whilst tearing apart the myth of religious neutrality in politics and the lie of a neutral secular public square. He also leaves you in a place where the gospel cannot be reduced just to personal salvation – it has implications for all of life.

In *Ruler of Kings*, Joe outlines the disease, prescribes the medicine, and encourages the Christian to stand up and boldly offer what we have - the only viable, rationally defensible answers to the world of the East and the West, the North and the South – that God's Revelation is the source of all truth, and that is not just soteriological but cosmological.

Jesus Christ is sovereign over all. All of creation and all the nations belong to Him.

Christ, not man, is King. Jesus is the Ruler of Kings. The Alpha and the Omega. Amen.

Andrea Williams

INTRODUCTION

Throughout the history of the church the question of the Christian's relationship to political authority has been a matter of discussion and debate. From the apostolic era, Christians have taught that Jesus Christ is king over all the earth and all the kingdoms of men, and that all the nations will ultimately bow in universal acknowledgment of His rule (cf. Ps. 2; Ps. 110; Phil. 2). Before that glorious day comes, we must understand – and live in – a world where human governments often do not acknowledge the Lordship of Jesus Christ. Positioned as we are historically against the backdrop of unprecedented restrictions on civil liberties in the West – including the forced closure of churches and restrictions on worship services in the wake of a virus – during the year of my writing this book there has been a not altogether surprising surge of popular interest in questions of church and state amongst Christians. This book seeks to make sense of three vital issues central to the realm of politics and civil government. It is by no means exhaustive; however, I believe that grasping these three issues in a biblically informed way provides the crucial lens for understanding the broader question of the Christian's role in and responsibility toward civil government.

First, I consider the late-modern phenomenon of secular intellectualism in the West and what has more recently been called the cult of the expert, examining the human tendency to shift great decision-making power to an intellectual elite in the belief that expertise in one isolated area equips one to lead and order life in many or all areas. From there I move to discuss the related issues of globalism and utopianism – two infernal ideologies pushed by a contemporary intellectual elite that go back as far as the Tower of Babel, and which manifest regularly in world history. Finally, I discuss both the inescapable fact and character of authority, and present in some detail what I believe is a scripturally rooted model for approaching the question of politics and church-state relations. My perspective is grounded in what is known as the sphere sovereignty model. This view is drawn from a rich tradition with a venerable legacy and is far from original to me. However, it is barely known or appreciated in the English-speaking world, and I am convinced that recent history and the troubling direction of political life today behoves a fresh recovery of this biblical vision for a new generation. If I can demonstrate to the reader in these pages the truth, value, and relevance of the Lordship of Jesus Christ for political life, and inspire the faithful to apply His sovereignty in our everyday interactions as believers, with the state, I will be very content.

Joseph Boot

Chapter 1

THE RULE OF CHRIST OR CULT OF THE EXPERT

The Problem Stated

A sober look at contemporary Western thought in the wake of both the Renaissance and the Enlightenment reveals that René Descartes' dictum remains as relevant as ever: "There is nothing so absurd or incredible that it has not been asserted by one philosopher or another." Because ideas have consequences, the ideas of thinkers and philosophers are eventually applied in cultural life. If these are not made subject to the Word of God, they can have disastrous outcomes because they manifest fallen man's rebellion against God's law-order. Today, we live in an era of perpetual revolution manifest by an intense intellectual activism in all cultural and political life. This requires, indeed demands, a distinctly Christian response. But herein lies a serious problem. From where can that Christian response come? What is the basis and *foundation* of a distinctly Christian response to the socio-political crisis of our time? That question is the subject of this book.

The Self-Anointed

Because of the steady triumph of pagan humanism in the West, the modern world has seen the re-emergence of many archaic oddities, one of which is a self-anointed elite class – the *intelligentsia* – a secular substitute for pastor and priest. The first truly modern intellectual, Jean-Jacques Rousseau, set a recognizable tone for the emergence of a self-righteous secular elite, making much of loving an abstraction called "the people," freeing them from the shackles of civilization and tradition, and establishing their "general will." But in the end, he could not disguise his disdain for humanity and likened the masses of ordinary people to "a stupid, pusillanimous invalid."[1]

A more recent defining example of this new class – still celebrated amongst cultural elites today – is George Bernard Shaw, the Irish playwright and public intellectual prominent in the first half of the twentieth century. Beyond writing plays, Shaw held forth on all kinds of cultural and political subjects and made grand sweeping pronouncements about his fellow human beings. Like many British intellectuals of the era, he was a Fabian socialist who nonetheless regarded ordinary working people as contemptible with "no right to live." He wrote, "I should despair if I did not know that they will all die presently, and that there is no need on earth why they should be replaced by people like themselves."[2] Shaw was also an admirer of dictators and political dictatorships precisely because he resented ordinary people influencing culture, believing they could not make sensible decisions. On leaving London for an African vacation in 1935, he remarked, "It is nice to go for a holiday and know that Hitler has settled everything so well in Europe."[3] Though Hitler's antisemitism eventually made it untenable for Shaw to support the national socialism of the Nazis, he remained keen on Stalin and the Soviet dictatorship.[4]

Jean-Paul Sartre, another twentieth-century Western intellectual with a massive cult following – well-known for seducing his young female philosophy students with the help of his lover, Simone de Beauvoir – like Shaw, frequently involved himself in cultural and political affairs of which he clearly had no adequate understanding. A man addicted to fornication, alcohol and barbiturates, Sartre proved incapable of maintaining relationships with male intellectual peers who might actually challenge him, and like his radical compatriots, was unable to bring himself to condemn Stalinism or the Communist Party – though he remained gregariously anti-American. He was still publicly defending the Soviets in the 1950s and warmly praising Mao's China. For Sartre, the remnants of an existing Christian political order in the West was simply 'institutionalized violence' that required 'intellectual activism' and 'necessary violence' to overthrow it.[5] In our own time, a majority of Western intellectuals have followed in the wake of thinkers like Sartre and groups like the Frankfurt School, hastening Western culture down into ever deeper levels of depravity, confusion, irrationality and self-immolation.[6] We are forced to ask as Christians, what has gone wrong?

The Foundation of Wisdom

It is a regularly observed phenomenon that many otherwise brilliant people appear utterly bereft of wisdom or judgment in the vital affairs of cultural and political life. In response to such imprudence and recklessness, this short work is an effort to articulate a foundation for a distinctly Christian view of politics. In order to do that, and to solve the paradox of cultural and political folly amongst much of the intelligentsia, it is first critical to realize that all cultural and political thought inescapably rests on a given foundation – one religious worldview or another is the frequently unacknowledged basis of all forms of political philosophy. Ultimately, from the scriptural standpoint, either Christ and His Word-revelation provides that foundation, or else the thinking of elites and their revolutionary ideals will assume the role of biblical authority. In the older testament, the great Hebrew thinker, politician and teacher, King Solomon, gives us the key to understanding why being intellectually gifted is no guarantee of true insight, wisdom or sound judgment: "The fear of the LORD is the *beginning* of knowledge; fools despise wisdom and discipline ... for the Lord gives wisdom; from His mouth come knowledge and understanding" (Prov. 1:7, 2:6). If the true *foundation* of wisdom is missing, if the *principal part* of knowledge is neglected, then any knowledge structure built upon it is inherently unstable. It may appear elegant and well-proportioned, but when the winds of the real world blow against it, it will be found wanting.

Clearly, intellect, intelligence and wisdom do not always coincide, are certainly not identical, and should never be conflated. A person may have the ability to grasp complex ideas (intellect) and even have the capacity to understand their relevant implications for a given area of thought (intelligence), but *wisdom* is of another character altogether. As Thomas Sowell points out, "wisdom is the rarest quality of all – the ability to combine intellect, knowledge, experience and judgment in a way to produce a coherent understanding. Wisdom is the fulfilment of the ancient admonition, 'With all your getting, get understanding.'"[7]

Intellectuals, Reason and Worldview

In the occupational construction of political and cultural ideas, the modern intellectual is usually (there are always exceptions) a person who claims allegiance to a *particular kind* of thinking and a commitment to the use of certain analytical tools and evaluative frameworks. Within these frameworks, ideas that are viewed as progressive or nuanced, novel, enlightened or artistically complex, tend to be applauded whereas 'traditional' ideas are largely dismissed as reactionary, simplistic or outmoded.[8] I remember some years ago a friend who was studying at a Christian university made the traditional assertion that Moses was the author of the first five books of the Bible, to which the instructor replied in a kind of stage whisper "what year is this?" It is perhaps not surprising that few openly and authentically Christian thinkers are welcomed into the exclusive chambers of orthodox intellectual elites.

In contemporary academia, this exclusivity, resting upon a claim of intellectual superiority, presupposes an idea going back to the Enlightenment – that there is an autonomous standard of self-regulating thought (i.e., secular *reasoning)*, protected by an elite class, before which all ideas must present themselves for judgment. Here we encounter the philosophical assumption that human thinking can function as the *lawgiver* of the world, prescribing *from thought* a law to nature. This claim of radical autonomy involving the idea of freedom from anything coming from outside the human subject is the basic idea of Western humanism since the Renaissance. It implies a total rejection of a divinely given *order for* creation. Contemporary trends in this form of thinking that now dominate our culture hold to a *social construction* theory of reality – we can *create* the world we live in by our thought and language, right down to our sexuality and identity. Today we see it expressed throughout the humanities, in economics, politics and law. It is not unusual for intellectuals to then protect these various judgments of their enlightened thought with the claim of *neutrality*, while those who disagree are regarded as uninformed, prejudiced, or hopelessly *biased.*

However, to make this appeal to a supposed *neutrality*, the basis of which is nothing but an established consensus amongst elites, is to assert that our rational behaviour is *self-normed.* This is something the true Christian is obligated to reject because, from a scriptural standpoint, the criteria for rational communication are *given with creation,* and *hold* for all rational pursuits. The criteria for meaningful discourse cannot be *derived* from the participants but must *hold* for them if there are to be universal normative standards for rational behavior. However, such an assertion of universal normative standards for thinking immediately threatens the pretended *autonomy* of the secular intellectual's thought – including his political thought. In other words, the question arises, how can human thinking be a *law unto itself* if it is bound by normative standards given with creation? Both convictions cannot be true at the same time.

To make this point clearer, it is important to recognize that there is a difference between a *norm or law*, and that which is being *subject* to that norm or law. For example, there is a law for the functioning of human cells, but the various individual cells are not identical with the *law for* the cell, neither do they generate that law, because laws are the *conditions which hold* for the existence of something. In a similar way our thinking and discourse (analytical and logical activities) are being *subjected* to norms constantly – in fact political debate presupposes that subjection. The crucial issue becomes: what is the *nature* of those norms? Are they *generated* by the thought of elites (i.e., laws *for* rational thought and thought itself are identical) or are they divinely created, supra-individual normative standards? With this question we are confronted with what the South African philosopher Danie Strauss calls "direction-giving ultimate commitments transcending the realm of rationality itself, since they are embedded in some or other world-and-life-view."[9] This immediately exposes the *non-neutrality* of all thought and shows that replacing revelation with a prevailing *trust* in autonomous 'reason' is not itself rational, but makes its appeal to beliefs and convictions that transcend the rational aspect of life.

Another important observation relevant to this discussion is that logical principles themselves do not provide the *grounds* for believing the *content* of certain arguments to be true or false; they can only help determine if the structure of a given argument is valid i.e., whether or not certain fallacies are present. As Karl Popper once put it, "[Since] all arguments must proceed from assumptions, it is plainly impossible to demand that all assumptions should be based on arguments." Which is simply to say, we already have to *believe* in something to begin to *justify* something else. Christians must always keep in mind that it is not thinking that thinks, but *human beings* – who are much more than their analytical function – that think. All human beings nurture basic beliefs and religious motives that give direction to their thinking, shaping the socio-political vision they advocate, and which inescapably inform the socio-political solutions they offer. As Thomas Sowell points out:

> Intellectuals do not simply have a series of isolated opinions on a variety of subjects. Behind those opinions is usually some coherent *over-arching conception of the world*, a social vision. Intellectuals are like other people in having visions – some intuitive sense of how the world works, what causes what... At the heart of the social vision prevalent among contemporary intellectuals is the belief that there are 'problems' created by existing institutions and that 'solutions' to these problems can be excogitated by intellectuals. This vision is both a vision of society and a vision of the role of intellectuals within society.[10]

The conception of the world which is dominant in our time has a lineage which stretches back via the Enlightenment to the Renaissance in its revival of pagan Greek thought. For a time, the biblical movement of the Reformation pushed back against this essentially neo-pagan tide by confronting people with the living God and His Word in its central religious significance. But with the protracted religious wars, disillusionment set in regarding the Christian church and so humanism revived and was emboldened by its new alliance with the rise of modern science – despite the development of the sciences being indebted to and dependent upon an essentially biblical view of reality.[11] The subsequent Enlightenment era doubled down on the assumptions of the Renaissance and as a movement had much wider and deeper penetration into the various aspects of people's lives. Christian resistance to the spread of unbelief again appeared with the evangelical Great Awakening. As is clear from the journals, letters and writings of the great men of that remarkable revival, though the period saw incredible fruit in evangelism and the development of personal piety, it lacked the rigour and theological depth of the Reformation era and generally missed the cultural scope of *application* for the Word seen amongst the Puritans. It gave pre-eminent attention to individual salvation of the soul with very little said about the cultural and political life of the nations. The later twentieth century development of Christian Bible colleges and seminaries (and in many cases Christian universities) did not have a root-and-branch reformation in thought and culture in view, but the protection and training of youth for a particular denomination or doctrinal loyalty. H. Evan Runner's analysis is telling:

> Failing to confront humanism in any central and comprehensive way, the Evangelical Revival stemmed the revolutionary tide less than the Reformation had done, and in fewer places. The Western world was rapidly becoming post-Christianly pagan. By the middle of the nineteenth century the educated class of Europe had broken overwhelmingly with any Christian point of view. In this way we can understand that humanism has been the dominant cultural driving force or mind in modern Western civilization, which, by taking possession of the hearts of untold millions, and by gaining control of our centres of authority and education, has undergone development and been given expression in and through the successive experiences of western men...Protestants came to withdraw either into a very restricted world of theological argument and investigation or, pietistically, into their private personal lives of 'devotion,'

failing to understand that the Word of God was given as light under which man was to live his life by on this earth…In none of the Protestant groups was the central "word" of Christ taking on flesh and blood as it was being *related to the conditions of our creaturely existence* in the continuing experiences of men through the modern centuries.[12]

Few things could be clearer in the early part of the twenty-first century than the urgent need for a comprehensive, scripturally rooted development of the *Christian mind*, and the application of this perspective to all of life, including the sphere of the state and political life. The Christian mind must not look at the world as the unbelieving thinker does – as a conundrum to be reduced to manageable basic components and "built anew" by our cognitive efforts. Nor must we regard our inherited institutions as the root of all evil in need of revolutionizing in terms of the euphoric visions of intellectuals. Sin is buried deep in the heart of man himself, not rooted in human institutions that can simply be reimagined by man's autonomous idea to cleanse away evil (Matt. 15:18-20).

With this in view, we will explore why the gospel of Christ must not be regarded or treated as an inspirational 'idea' that offers immediate 'solutions' to various societal 'problems.' Rather, the gospel declares the kingdom and power of God manifest in both the creative and redemptive work of Jesus Christ, which transforms the heart of man, and in so doing makes a *new creature* out of him. The fruit of this transformation is a Spirit-given vision for Christ's kingdom to come and the will of the Father to be done in every aspect of creation. This God-ordained vision calls not for self-anointed *experts*, but for faithful and Spirit-anointed *servants* committed to the Law-Word of God for creation and culture and to excellence in each sphere of life for the glory of God.

A Basic Difference Between Christian and Secular Political Thought

We have already seen that the *foundation* for thinking between the Christian and non-Christian is radically different. One professes *autonomy (self-law)*, the other *theonomy (God's law)* – meaning a total surrender to the Law-Word of Christ in creation and Scripture, in whom are hidden all the treasures of wisdom and knowledge (Col. 2:3). This theonomic orientation is lucidly described by Runner:

> God's Law is God's Word. Because God is God, His every Word is Law. From the very first words of the Bible we hear, "And God said, Let there be" this and that. All such creative words are the Law. The Law is what causes creatures and the whole creation to hang together; it determines the conditions of all creaturely existence. It is itself concentrated in the religious law of life: Walk before me according to my commandments and live. Here we have the heart of the creation. The Law determines what it means to live before God, or to die before God.[13]

In the fantasy of autonomy, the modern intellectual, embodying the spirit of our times, essentially pretends to the realization of a new priesthood within society, incarnating a new source of ultimate authority by setting aside *the* prophet, priest and king – Jesus Christ and His kingdom people. Such intellectuals as a class tend to regard themselves as representing a *concentration point* of human knowledge and understanding. As secular bishops, they *mediate* their ideas by influencing and shaping those who will then proclaim and disseminate their vision for them – a kind of substitute clergy in media and education, law, *politics* and arts known as the *intelligentsia*. Only by a deliberate and purposeful act of submission to God's Word-revelation can the Christian thinker avoid the conceits of a godless intelligentsia. This submission to God's Word must in turn lead to the development of a coherent and systematic

Christian world-and-life view that serves the kingdom of God by mediating not man's word, but the Word of a comprehensive gospel, to every aspect of human life in all creation.

Second, because of a submission to God and His Word-revelation, not only is the Christian thinker totally subject to Scripture, he or she is also accountable to the normative structure of created reality as God has ordained it by His Law-Word. This means that true Christian thinking is willingly and joyfully submitted to God's Word in creation and does not attempt to remake it after human imagination. Rather than submitting to revelation, from the time of Plato and Aristotle, intellectuals have tended to engage in abstract thought-experiments making playthings of the lives of people in the name of their greater insight or apprehension of 'natural law.' From Plato's *Republic* and Aristotle's *Politics* to Sir Thomas More's *Utopia* and Karl Marx's *Das Kapital*, Western civilization has been profoundly impacted by different styles of social thought-experiment that deal with people, politics and culture in the *abstract* – as these thinkers would *prefer* persons and the world to be – but which do not really grapple with the world and history in its *givenness*. Outside of the laboratory of the mind, however, such thought-experiments have real-life consequences. The atheistic materialism of Marx's thought, with its abstract revolutionary masses throwing off the evils of wage labor and private property, supposedly leading mankind toward total freedom in a stateless and work-free world, has cost millions of people their lives. During the age of the Enlightenment *philosophes*, Rousseau attacked Christian civilisation and idealized the 'noble savage' whilst abandoning all of his own children to a hospice where they almost certainly died. In more recent decades John Rawls described a 'veil of ignorance' in contractarian political theories of society, positing imaginary worlds free from metaphysical beliefs or cultural history. All such abstractions are erroneous in large measure because they are inattentive to the human condition and social reality.

One of the important differences between the occupation of intellectuals and that of the engineer is that engineers find themselves constantly *accountable to the real world* if they make mistakes. If I make a mistake with a historical or philosophical reference in one of my articles or lectures, I may get a kind (or angry) email from a reader pointing out my error, but if my brother Daniel who is a heating engineer (designing and installing complex heating systems in commercial properties) makes a serious mistake, real college dorm rooms or somebody's office will be flooded, or catch fire, or explode. There is an immediate accountability here in the concrete world of experience – an external standard of accountability. An engineer whose designs and work prove to be a repeated failure will not long be in the industry. Yet if an intellectual has a grand new idea, happens to be or become influential and the idea is applied but fails, that thinker is often seen as a brave pioneer or prophet out of time. At other times, as so clearly manifest in Marxist social theory, the blame for the failure of the thinker's ideas is placed on 'society' or others' 'faulty interpretation or application,' and not infrequently on the stupidity of the masses for the philosophy not working.

Take current gender theories like those of Judith Butler which assert that sex is 'fictive' i.e., a creation of *political language regimes* forming perceptions of the body as having male and female identity, but which are in fact just forms of oppression. Or consider feminist theories seeking to level all distinctions between men and women, and various other forms of deconstructionist critical theory. External tests in the real world that would be applied to the engineer don't seem to apply here. The only test that seems to matter is what other feminists, queer theorists and critical theorists amongst the intelligentsia think;

do they find the ideas original, appropriately subversive of authority, or progressive and imaginative? When the lives, education and socio-economic future of children, families and society are destroyed by the application of these intellectuals' near-unintelligible word games, the blame is placed on societal taboos, the patriarchal family, traditional institutions, structural inequality and systemic racism for things not working out well. The givenness of creation and God's Law-Word for society, which is what invariably frustrates their purpose, is dismissed as simply a power structure to be revolted against.

Consider again the various shades of Marxist political philosophy that have been tried numerous times on various continents with the same devastating and tragic results; the repeated failure doesn't stop intellectuals committed to an abstract ideology continuing to venerate Marxist social theory whilst blaming a faulty application or nuance of interpretation for the economic devastation or vicious death of multitudes. This is because their criteria for judgment is essentially *internal,* not *external* – which is to say man must *prescribe,* not discover and *acknowledge,* the normative structures for human life. Thus, in the name of intellectual freedom, unaccountability becomes a hallmark of the occupation of both the intellectual and the intelligentsia which follows them. The noted British intellectual, John Stuart Mill, went as far as to argue that intellectuals should be free even from social standards, all the while setting those standards for others.[14] It is existing institutions and traditions, norms and standards that must change to accommodate the intellectuals' ideas, not the thinker who must be subject to laws and norms in the created world.

In marked contrast, the Christian must submit their thinking to Scripture and explore the various spheres of the creation order as *revelation* from God. Together, these have a 'norming' impact on Christian thought, giving concrete direction to the believer's labors in every sphere – including the political. The thought-products of Christians can then be judged by and made accountable to an external standard, just as the prophets in Scripture were judged in terms of their faithfulness to the Word of God and accuracy of their description of God's historical activities.

The Cult of the Expert or the Worship of Christ

One of the besetting sins of professional intellectuals as a class is believing that, because they have a particular depth of knowledge or strong ability in a given area, they can then generalize their narrow knowledge and ability into the notion of their own superior wisdom and judgement for life in general. Frequently disregarding the everyday, non-theoretical and mundane knowledge of ordinary people in the real world, central socio-political planning is taken on by the 'experts' – a particular kind of intellectual – as part of a broader intelligentsia who believe they alone are qualified to guide and shape society. As Thomas Sowell has rightly pointed out, "Intellectuals have seen themselves not simply as an elite – in the passive sense in which large landowners, rentiers, or holders of various sinecures might qualify as elites – but as an *anointed* elite, people with a mission to lead others in one way or another toward better lives."[15]

We have seen this modern cult at work during the era of the Covid-19 related crisis, with intellectuals in the fields of virology, statistics and computer modelling wheeled out by politicians to proclaim that civil liberties should be suspended for months on end, while prophesying that life can never return to the way it was before if we are to have a safe and healthy future. Because they are the 'experts,' few pause to ask what qualifies a virologist, computer modeller or statistician to make far-reaching social, political and juridical decisions that profoundly affect millions of people around the world, including those of us in ostensibly free societies. But according to the politicians we must all be guided by the 'experts.'

Another good example is seen in the field of economics – a bamboozling subject for the uninitiated as literal 'magic tricks' are performed by financial experts. For most of us ordinary mortals, we assume that paper money must *represent* a specific value of something concrete that has a generally agreed worth. Therefore, a certain number of dollars will buy me a certain number of potatoes (the paper being monetized wealth for the purpose of trade). Countries in which trust in their currency evaporates – as was seen in Zimbabwe, the former Soviet Union and is taking place now in Venezuela – soon find that a wheelbarrow full of paper money will not buy them a loaf of bread because their money is suspected of being no longer backed by something real and reliable, inflation having pushed the price of goods that much higher. Yet we are told by experts today that modern economies do not need to be backed by gold and other precious metals but can function safely simply on debt and government promises. The political answer to financial crises is therefore not 'austerity' and a balanced budget, but more and more public spending and *stimulus* to grow the economy. Stimulus means quantitative easing (that is, printing more and more paper money), with governments accumulating more and more debt, supported by the promise of future tax revenues and economic growth (GDP). As money gets cheaper due to its increased availability, keeping interest rates artificially low, many people borrow more, whilst the savings of others are effectively devalued (money now being worth less). However, markets inevitably aware of the problem will be concerned with looming runaway inflation. The sustainability of this model is therefore predicated on the ideas of unending economic growth and trust in government experts manipulating economic reality.

Thus, for most Western governments, the idea of a balanced budget has gone the way of the dodo.

Whatever we make of this, the point is that economic and monetary policy is not value-neutral but equally driven by the thinking of expert-intellectuals who are not simply accountants and economists but people shaping life and culture in terms of a *worldview*, believing they are uniquely qualified to guide society. As Stephen D. King notes:

> The idea that monetary policy is politically neutral is a convenient fiction rather than a reflection of reality. Yet it is often only during periods of economic and social upheaval that the fiction is exposed. Today, monetary policy works not so much by reinvigorating the economy but, instead, by redistributing wealth and income: it is no more than a stealthy form of redistributive taxation.[16]

There is nothing truly new here. Whether the area is economic life, law, medicine, education, politics or some other area of cultural import, from the time of the Pharaoh's magicians and the Persian magi, kings, emperors and political leaders have surrounded themselves with a cadre of 'experts' to both give counsel and to act as a convenient means of shifting blame if things went wrong. Of course the intellectuals of the ancient and classical world did not enjoy the same levels of unaccountability that the modern expert enjoys. If you misinterpreted Pharaoh's dream or that of the king of Babylon, you might be executed. But whether they were called satraps or soothsayers, advisers or counselors, scholars or magi, they were the public intellectuals of their era and frequently functioned as a priestly class guiding the religious and political life of the people. These thinkers, however, were invariably fumbling in the darkness, disconnected from the revealed covenants of promise and often oblivious to the clarity of God's revelation in creation. Unless any expert intellectual is willingly subject to

Christ and His Word-revelation, even when they stumble across God's creational laws and norms in their work, they will consistently fail to properly apply what they have learned in terms of the fullness of the wisdom of God – for as we have seen, intellect, intelligence and wisdom are not same thing.

Prophetic Thinking in Politics

Nonetheless, from a scriptural standpoint, there remains an important role for the person whose work-product is ideas – there is a legitimate task for the intellectual in cultural and political life. In the Bible we notice it is God who gives his servant Joseph *wisdom* in pagan Egypt to understand the times, advise and serve in political office and correctly interpret dreams given by Him to Pharaoh for the deliverance of both Egypt and Joseph's family from famine (Acts 7: 9-16). Along with the famed king Solomon, who gave us the books of Ecclesiastes, Proverbs and Song of Solomon, and whose careful observations and wise applications of God's Law-Word in creation and Scripture brought even the queen of Sheba to hear him (1 Kings 10:1-9), perhaps the best example of a believing political thinker and public intellectual in Scripture is that of Daniel. Because of his lineage and gifts, he is specifically recruited into an elite school for the ancient equivalent of experts or intellectuals – scholars and thinkers among whom some would give guidance to society and government (Dan. 1:3-6). Along with some noble friends from Judah (Shadrach, Meshach and Abednego), noted for their resistance to idolatry to the point of being cast into a fiery furnace, Daniel is identified as having real potential as an advisor in the king's court for the government of the people.

These men determined to honor God in their occupation from the start. As a result, the Bible tells us, "God gave these four young men knowledge and understanding in every kind of literature and wisdom. Daniel also understood visions and dreams of every kind ... no one was found equal to Daniel...so they began to serve in the king's court. In every matter of wisdom and understanding that the king consulted them about, he found them ten times better than all the diviner-priests and mediums in his entire kingdom" (Dan. 1:17-21). Daniel and his friends went on to distinguish themselves, finding high position in the realm and government of Babylon, where in God's providence they exercised profound influence for the *kingdom of God* from the head of state down. This was possible because they were granted knowledge, wisdom and understanding by the Lord Himself and determined to obey God's commands and serve diligently to His glory.

These men were intimately acquainted with the truth that the *fear of the Lord is the beginning of wisdom*. The other intellectuals and government advisors lacked such understanding and prophetic perception because the foundation of their thought was wanting. They lacked insight into the normative structure of creation because they were unsubmitted to the Law-Word of God. The advantage that Daniel and his friends enjoyed should be even more apparent with the Christian thinker who is self-consciously subject to God's Word in Scripture and creation. In Christ all the treasures of wisdom and knowledge are hid (Col. 2:3), meaning that the Christian thinker can avoid the pitfalls and mistakes of a godless intelligentsia by apprehending and appreciating all things in their true context, from within a scriptural world-and-life view. This makes the Christian mind unique, containing a prophetic power that comprehends all creation as an instantiation of the Word of God.

In the final analysis, as valuable as the insights of all those who make careful study of any of the marvelous functions of creation can be, our trust and hope will either be in Christ and His Word-revelation or the expertise of autonomous man. The history of every era is littered with the false prophecy of the intelligentsia of that time. To place ultimate trust in the 'ideas' of people is a fool's gambit, like the unwise man who built his house upon the sands of lawlessness. But to put our trust in Christ and His Law-Word is to be wise and build our house on the rock (Matt. 7:21-27). Men's ideas come and go, but the Word of the Lord stands forever. The gospel of the kingdom is not man's tyrannous political idea, but the redemptive and restorative Word of God for every area of life. Only in this Word is there life and freedom for human society. In the memorable words of the historian Paul Johnson, "we must at all times remember what intellectuals habitually forget…the worst of all despotisms is the heartless tyranny of ideas."[17]

Contrary to popular opinion, Scripture does give Christians a mandate to apply the wisdom of God's Law-Word to political life rather than relying on the ideas of godless people. To neglect this task is to faithlessly abandon our society and culture to despotism and tyranny.

Chapter 2

GLOBALIST UTOPIA VERSUS BIBLICAL NATIONHOOD

Kingdom and Utopia

Having analyzed the contemporary cult of the expert, we are now ready to examine in detail the principal political vision that has dominated the thought of the intellectual class in the West for several centuries. That ideology is utopianism, manifest most recently in the pervasive aspiration of globalism.

There are few more odious men that emerge from the pages of European history than the first truly 'modern' intellectual, the professional hypocrite, Jean-Jacques Rousseau, famed author of *The Social Contract*. David Hume, who knew him well, by bitter experience called him "a monster who saw himself as the only important being in the universe." Voltaire thought him "a monster of vanity and vileness." Diderot, after knowing him for many years described him as "deceitful, vain as Satan, ungrateful, cruel, hypocritical, and full of malice." He is perhaps most tellingly summed up in the words of the woman who he claimed was his only love, Sophie d' Houdetot. In old age she said, "He was ugly enough to frighten me and love did not make him more attractive. But he was a pathetic figure and I treated him with gentleness and kindness. He was an interesting madman."[18] Following Plato, Rousseau was a utopian dreamer, yet without doubt was a debauched narcissist who, whilst presuming to lecture others on education, family and state, abandoned all five of his own children in infancy to a hospice where they almost certainly died. Yet in many ways, despite his infantile and vile character, his masochism and exhibitionism, his thought paved the way for the French Revolution and influenced the Russian Revolution, as well as playing a real role in inspiring both communist and fascist regimes in the twentieth century. He was an intellectual forerunner of Karl Marx and saw in the state the key to Utopia. The historian Paul Johnson has written:

> Rousseau's state is not merely authoritarian: it is also totalitarian, since it orders every aspect of human activity, thought included. Under the social contract, the individual was obliged to "alienate himself, with all his rights, to the whole community" (i.e. the state) ... The function of the social contract, and the state it brought into being, was to make man whole again: "Make man one, and you will make him as happy as he can be".... You must, therefore, treat citizens as children and control their upbringing and thoughts, planting, "the social law in the bottom of their hearts." They then become "social men by their natures and citizens by their inclinations; they will be one, they will be good, they will be happy, and their happiness will be that of the republic".... He did not use the word 'brainwash,' but he wrote: "Those who control a people's opinions control its actions." Such control is established by treating citizens, from infancy, as children of the state, trained to "consider themselves only in their relationship to the body of the state" ...he moved the political process to the very centre of human existence, by making the legislator, who is also a pedagogue, into the new Messiah, capable of solving all human problems by creating New Men.[19]

If Rousseau's ideas here sound remarkably contemporary it is because his utopian thought has so decisively shaped our current political and social order. Today's cultural Marxists who are busy with their ideological subversion and demoralization of the West in the name of social justice, have Rousseau to thank for their core ideas. It is therefore of tremendous concern when anti-Christian utopianism is imported into ostensibly Christian cultural theology in the name of the reign or kingdom of God – here a socio-political religion replaces Christianity. When developing a distinctly Christian political vision it is imperative that Christians understand the difference between utopianism and the kingdom of God, lest they be found advancing the cause of other gods and another faith.

The Utopian Imperative

The term *Utopia* originates with Thomas More's ideal society and it means "no place." More, who was sainted by the Roman Catholic church in 1935, was far from biblical in his thinking. His famous treatise is a plea for the abolition of private property and the establishment of communism. More's work is anti-Christian and subversive to the church positing 'nature' as the measure of reality and virtue, and the state as man's re-creator, provider and preserver. As for all utopians, *unity* was More's supreme virtue. Peace comes through the state – the humanly-wrought oneness into which man is absorbed. More saw himself as an elite ruler in a new order in which men would be manipulated to remove all social divisions. It is not surprising that Lenin found inspiration in More's ideas.[20]

True Christian orthodoxy *cannot* produce such utopian illusions. The creator, redeemer God, in his complete word, has declared the future of his Kingdom and rule, established by his will and power. Since God governs history, the Christian, in faith, obedience and confidence, moves toward God's predestined and ordained future (Eph. 1:3–14; Prov. 16:4). The triune, sovereign Lord, who by his providence and power sustains all things (Heb. 1:1–3), is the one in whom the Christian trusts. Bereft of such security, the non-believer must posit an entirely different worldview. Utopianism, which denies God's sovereign and predestinating purpose, is more than a political idea; it is a philosophy of life, a religious theology. Instead of seeing man's environment as a good (though fallen) creation under the providence of God, utopianism perceives man to be in a chaotic universe that perpetually threatens to crush him. The noted British utopian dreamer, Julian Huxley, encapsulates the modern humanistic temper:

> So far as we can see [the universe] rules itself...even if a god does exist behind or above the universe as we experience it, we can have no knowledge of such a power: the actual gods of historical religions are only the personifications of impersonal facts of nature and of facts of our inner mental life.[21]

In this view, 'nature' is as capricious as the pagan gods of Greco-Roman mythology or as man's own inner life of evil thoughts. As Thomas Molnar puts it, "our vision of the universe inevitably influences our vision of society and, hence, our organization of society. If the universe is hostile to us, we conceive of society, our little universe, as also hostile."[22] Having jettisoned the God of the Bible, utopians are confronted by a threatening world of flux – perpetual change without a source of constancy. They see no God to give purpose, direction and order to life. This world of chaos in which man's 'freedom' runs wild jeopardizes its own existence by its unpredictability. Man lives in terror, a victim of fate and full of self-pity. In a world without God man experiences an insatiable desire for control, rooted in the hope that man can be liberated from unpredictability into the true freedom of necessity! As J. B. S. Haldane, a Marxist utopian, put it, "There is no supernatural and nothing metaphysical...freedom is the recognition of necessity. This is a paradox, but a truth."[23] But when man theoretically frees himself from the sovereignty of God, he quickly discovers a serious problem: absolute autonomy (self-law) leads logically to total anarchy of thought and to social chaos. Since chaos is not a tolerable basis for a civilization, to avoid this disaster the individual is inevitably plunged into a *collectivity* that will *assume the role* of God in creating, predestinating, saving, guiding and providing for the newly liberated man. The new man-god is the collective agency for organizing man's liberty and salvation. This collective divinity is a Nebuchadnezzar-sized idol that steadily *lays claim to all the attributes of the God it has replaced.* The utopian devotee may not seem religious, since he rarely mentions God, judgement, salvation, heaven or hell. But he constantly formulates new doctrines, ceremonies and sacrifices. Huxley, the key writer of UNESCO's founding framework document, is explicit:

> If we translate salvation into terms of this world, we find that it means achieving *harmony* between different parts of our nature, including its subconscious depths and its rarely touched heights, and also achieving some satisfactory relation of adjustment between ourselves and the outer world, including not only the world of nature, but the social world of man. I believe it to be possible to "achieve salvation" in this sense, and right to aim at doing so, just as I believe it possible and valuable to achieve a sense of union with something bigger than our ordinary selves, even if that something be not a god but an extension of our narrow core to include in a single grasp ranges of outer experience and inner nature on which we do not ordinarily draw.[24]

Huxley blends secular terminology with the language of pagan spirituality. The union with something bigger than the self is the whole, the one, the ideal of man divinized in and by his unification with himself (nature). Huxley goes on to argue that purpose lies in 'science', namely the endless possibilities of the evolution of man by socialization, organization and technology, through which man gains *power over nature* (himself) to deliver and save himself from suffering and pain, (intolerable to all utopians, including those found in Eastern and pagan spirituality). The possible implications of such a utopian vision were foreseen by George Orwell in his dystopian novel *1984*, where he envisages the problem confronting all Utopian dreams – fallen man's *misdirected* exercise of power is demonic – only power for the sake of power is expressed when man usurps the prerogatives of God. Orwell has O'Brien declare in a noted passage:

Power is in inflicting pain and humiliation. Power is in tearing human minds to pieces and putting them together again in new shapes of your own choosing. Do you begin to see, then, what kind of world we are creating? It is the exact opposite of the stupid hedonistic Utopias that the old reformers imagined. A world of fear and treachery and torment, a world of trampling and being trampled upon, a world which will grow not less, but more merciless as it refines itself. Progress in our world will be progress toward more pain…already we are breaking down the habits of thought which have survived from before the revolution. We have cut the links between child and parent, and between man and man, and between man and woman. No one dares trust a wife or a child, or a friend any longer. But in the future there will be no wives and no friends. Children will be taken from their mothers at birth, as one takes eggs from a hen. The sex instinct will be eradicated. Procreation will be an annual formality like the renewal of a ration card…there will be no loyalty except loyalty toward the party. There will be no love except the love of Big Brother…there will be no art, no literature, no science. When we are omnipotent we shall have no more need of science. There will be no distinction between beauty and ugliness. There will be no curiosity, no employment of the process of life. All competing pleasures will be destroyed. But always – do not forget this Winston – always there will be the intoxication of power, constantly increasing and constantly growing subtler. Always at every moment, there will be the thrill of victory, the sensation of trampling on the enemy who is helpless. If you want a picture of the future, imagine a boot stamping on a human face – forever.[25]

Here we have a powerful image of man's sin coming to self-conscious realization where man, as the new divinity, gains the sensation of pseudo-omnipotence in the collectivist order. Playing at God, total terror and total destruction are the reality as the new man-god brings his perverse wrath to bear on the world. This is his route to godhood – the exercise of naked power. In a twist of morbid irony, Orwell demonstrates that power presupposes, and indeed requires, hierarchy, something that the utopian often overlooks in his pursuit of equality and unity. For power is the capacity to act, to effect a change on something, and the exercise of power necessarily requires an *other* to be acted upon. Whenever man sets out on a utopian project, he always starts with the anarchistic rejection of God and then proceeds to a re-making of man as nature (god) incarnate through the Parliament of man, the federation of the world, as Tennyson referred to it. The solution to man's disunity, his alienation from himself, is therefore seen in a collectivist order, and ultimately a world-state.

This concept reflects more than mere idealism or a minor substratum of Western thought. It appears as a logical necessity born of a lasting, deep religious hunger in those who have rejected the God of Scripture. Man needs order, certainty and salvation, and where Christ's governance is denied, man will attempt to mimic it. Wherever man has denied or rejected the transcendent God and sought instead an immanentized source and root of power, a *theology of state* has developed and a new doctrine of God has been fleshed out. Although explicitly theological language is often jettisoned, the new doctrine is expressed in the terminology of the social or scientific revolutionary or in that of the new occultist spirituality. All that impedes the utopian revolution is the propaganda of priests, the family and the church. Consequently orthodox Christianity is seen as the ultimate enemy of utopia. As J. L. Talmon expressed it, "The messianic trends [of the nineteenth century] considered Christianity as arch enemy...their own message of salvation was utterly incompatible with the true Christian doctrine, that of original sin, with its vision of history as the story of the fall, and its denial of man's power to attain salvation by his own exertions."[26] So, man has replaced Christ and His word, and needs a new doctrine of God and a new word. In this re-imagining process, he transfers the key attributes of God to man and his agencies. Because man is a sinner, these utopian schemes must always be dystopian in their outcomes. Let us now examine why.

A New Doctrine of God: The Unity of the Utopian Godhead

Justice

Utopian literature was one of the key markers of the beginning of the modern age, though Plato's *Republic* is basic to all such modern utopias. From Thomas More to Sir Francis Bacon, Tommaso Campanella and James Harrington, man dreamt of restoring paradise to the earth. The essential ingredient in making this a reality is that the state (personified by elite philosopher-kings) must be allowed to 'organize' society through technology (power) and scientific socialism, in terms of man's new conception of *justice*, which now means liberation from God. Justice is no longer located in God and his law, but in radical egalitarian levelling as the route to reunification. Where differences exist to any degree, this unity cannot be achieved. But why is inequality, moral differentiation, diversity and variety such a horror to man's utopian aspirations?

First, we must notice that the doctrine of God is inescapable. If man pretends God is dead, his need for the doctrine of God does not disappear, it is merely transferred from the transcendent to the immanent (within the world) realm. Now central to the doctrine of God is the *unity* of the godhead, for God cannot be divided against Himself! In the Christian faith, as revealed in Scripture and summarized in the ecumenical creeds of the church, we believe in one God in three persons in perfect relational unity, fully representative of each other, and equally ultimate. Satanically inspired thought always counterfeits these doctrines because they are inescapable categories to man as God's image-bearer. So interestingly, both the doctrine of God and the kingdom of God are counterfeited in utopianism. Second, the idea of *alienation* is critical to the utopian worldview because it suggests man is alienated from his true being. This idea is not new. It is as old as ancient Greek philosophy. In Plato and Aristotle, we are offered the form/matter scheme. According to Plato, Form or Idea produces the copies in the tangible world which are increasingly imperfect in proportion to their distance from the original.

Man is therefore alienated from the *idea* of man and as such cannot find unity with or within himself. Hegel's philosophy is critically important here in understanding the development of this concept in the West: Hegel's system regards man as condemned to externalize himself, to cease being pure consciousness. Every interpersonal relationship, every relationship with the state, every economic relationship and every relationship with God and religion is reification (objectivization) of man's subjective essence.[27] Here, man is steadily alienated from his true godhood simply by consciousness of anything outside himself – the essence of self being pure spirit or pure consciousness. This same idea is central to Buddhism and Hinduism, in which the goal of existence is re-absorption in the *one*, Brahma or Nirvana. The goal of pantheistic meditation (i.e. yoga) is to recognize the ultimate oneness and unity of all things, that distinctions are mere illusions. In Buddhism, the ultimate goal is pure consciousness which is unconsciousness –

the annihilation of the idea of self altogether. Thus in Hegel, West meets East intellectually, although the implications are developed in different ways. Hegel saw the differentiation manifest in history and the created order as scattered bits of 'god' (human consciousness, pure spirit) everywhere. Therefore, man can only realize himself (discover his godhood) by *reunification with the fragmented self.*

The quintessential utopian – and early disciple of Hegel – Karl Marx claimed to have solved this problem of fragmentation within the communist society. Marx held that man was alienated from nature (himself), but could become one with it through work, an action of *nature* manifesting itself through man. Nature is the object and man the subject, so a history created and controlled by industry was thought to reconcile subject and object (oneness). Nature (god) recreates itself by man's work, which expresses his *one essence* with nature. Nature, realized in man, is really god, yet doesn't realize it because it has been alienated from itself by the Christian theistic doctrines of God, man and the world. Man must become self-conscious, aware of being his own creator through work – a consciousness created by the re-making of nature through scientific socialism. When the working classes of the West failed to overthrow the bourgeoisie and establish a communist utopia, Marxism reconstituted itself in less immediate, but no less concrete terms as ecological and spiritualized socialism that seeks an androgynous, classless, discrimination – and distinction-less world of 'social justice' – a world ruled by a scientific, socialist, pagan elite.

Globalist Technocracy

In recent years, Marxism has displayed a globalist and distinctly technocratic character, with the pretence of being able to predict the future in a 'scientific' way. The move toward globalism is a natural and logical extension of Marxism, the idea of man's reason as 'law-giver' for all reality and its concomitant totalizing, centralizing ideology. By reason, man takes the world apart by reducing it to its supposed basic material components and reassembles or remakes it in terms of his own idea within the historical process; the whole of reality is to be viewed as the stuff of his creative force. With a global community potentially owning the production forces (i.e. human beings and means of production) societal alienation can be theoretically eliminated by changing production relations. Central to this change is technology. The potential of cybernetics (self-regulating systems/machines) means the possibility of liberating human beings from slavery to nature, in order to live creative lives and be completely themselves. So armed, man can save himself from servitude. Protestant 'capitalist' production relations (i.e. private property, sale and purchase, the biblical family structure and hierarchy, employers and employees, workers and owners etc.,) are a form of slavery and a hindrance to this progress and must be transcended and abolished.

As technology advances, history supposedly progresses in freedom as this 'alienation' is done away with. However, this 'Kingdom of Freedom' is not freedom as Christianity understands it. The progress of history is a constantly expanding range of controlled and regulated acts – society itself being conceived as a self-regulating system. The human being as a societal person (part of a collective) is thought of as the highest product of matter, caught up in a necessary historical process where one surrenders individual being. Only a socialist order (ultimately a global one), can realise this freedom of necessity.

By such a conception of the nature and role of technology, Marxist thought reduces man to *Homo Faber*, man the maker. Which is to say, man is reduced to technology and society to technocracy. Human existence is understood and accounted for entirely in its artificiality – human self-generation as a force for production or procreation. Egbert Schuurman summarises the Marxist view:

> [I]n Marxism, humanity as a species liberates itself, in and through technology, from all oppression and bondage, whether natural or societal. The unadulterated technological-active-historical society thereby becomes the authentic being of mankind. From the preceding it is apparent that for the Marxist, technology becomes a religion. Such a person believes that technological development brings progress that will issue in a kingdom of freedom. The reverse side of this kingdom of freedom is the elimination of the individual. Therefore, the freedom attained can never be anything more than societal freedom.[28]

Working hand in glove with the idea of a global technocracy is the utopian goal of equality, one of those words which Marxism invests with a radically revised meaning. If equality is the goal, it stands to reason that the current state of society is one of inequality – a state of affairs that must be corrected, and the process involves the development of a panoply of human rights for groups that demand not only equal opportunity but equal outcomes for all. This is the ideological root of all our contemporary 'liberation' movements – animal, ecological, oceanographic or any other stripe. The *sine qua non* of all victimhood is the planet or nature itself, standing proxy for all 'oppressed' groups everywhere. It is no longer the bourgeois oppressing the proletariat. Nature itself must be liberated in order for man to re-create himself. This liberation requires radical equalization in order to stop the white, Christian, capitalist plunderers. This schema alone will bring about social justice, and all who oppose this program are cast as the oppressors and the enemies of human liberation.

In all forms of Marxist thought, human consciousness is the supreme divinity. The idea of 'god' is retained only as the ideal of perfection, even though he has no concrete existence; god exists only potentially because it can concretize itself in socialist mankind. So, "we are confronted with this strange paradox: the Marxist utopian denies the existence of God, but he holds that man may become divine or may develop a combination of purity and power that will transcend any human form."[29] Essentially, Marxist man does believe in a kind of super-nature – collective man. This transcending of human form is achieved by scientific and technological work that accomplishes man's essential unity with nature. "When man conquers nature he acquires the decisive victory over himself; he possesses himself."[30] This new god, by industry, continues to create. By doing so he believes he defeats what to him is the problem of history: sin, suffering and laborious work.

The dominant utopian worldview then is evolutionary, pantheistic and materialistic. Spirit and matter are one or are in the inexorable process of becoming one. The individual is identified with everybody and everybody is then elevated to divinity. In order for the man-god to be reunited with itself, in order to achieve *the unity of the godhead*, socialization and *humanization* must take place. These *require the co-operation of all men* in all the common tasks laid down by 'science,' as well as the reduction of all things to the secular, to the human, defined by time and by this world alone, not in terms of God, His Word, or eternity. By vague philosophic abstractionism, secular theologies (whether religious liberalism or secular) make the notion of god so incomprehensible as to become meaningless. Human qualities are then blown up to cosmic proportions, ultimately asserting a 'universal mind,' and the results are called divine. For Teilhard de Chardin, for example, this is the *Omega Point*.[31] This is the occultic emergence of a united super mankind.

The confidence of many elites past and present has been in the unity of the new godhead – man. Bertrand Russell, widely regarded as one of the twentieth century's most important British intellectuals, was not only an atheist but an ardent utopian. He writes:

> It is the conquest of nature which has made possible a more friendly and co-operative attitude between human beings, and if rational men co-operated and used their scientific knowledge to the full, then the world could now secure the economic welfare of all.... International government, business organization, and birth control should make the world comfortable for everybody.... With the problem of poverty and destitution eliminated, men could devote themselves to the constructive arts of civilization – to the progress of science, the diminution of disease, the postponement of death, and the liberation of the impulses that make for joy.... Take first, international government. The necessity for this is patent to every person capable of political thought…when all the armed forces of the world are controlled by one world-wide authority, we shall have reached the stage in the relation of states which was reached centuries ago in the relations of individuals. Nothing less than this will suffice. The road to Utopia is clear; it lies partly through politics and partly through changes in the individual. As for politics, far the most important thing is the establishment of an international government.[32]

Though he formally repudiated communism, Russell believed in a world superstate with total power and a form of collectivism that would involve severe restrictions on human liberty including that cloak for murder and eugenics – 'birth control.' For him it was essential that man, as the new god of nature, must unite 'by love' if the conquest of nature is to be complete and death itself postponed or even defeated.

Love

This points us to the other critical ingredient in realizing the unity of the godhead – love! Man must be made to 'love' all men and for the utopian ideology this love means social justice. This must not be equated with love and justice in the biblical sense which entails the love of God and neighbour as the fulfilment of God's law (Lev. 19:18; Matt. 22:38–39; Rom. 13:10). Rather, since love of the living God is rejected, man must love the new god, collectivist man, with absolute and unswerving devotion. The God of Scripture is thus abandoned in favour of 'divine' interpersonal relationships. For there to be unity in the new godhead there must be total equality and equal ultimacy among all people which means loving all things. This means that there can be no *discrimination* in regard to anything. To insist there is a *moral* difference between people and their actions in terms of right and wrong, truth and falsehood or good and evil, as an standard transcending merely human ideas, constitutes *discrimination*. In this worldview to discriminate against anything (except Christianity) is a contradiction of the utopian's most basic premise – oneness or total unity. Anything that cannot be universally embraced by all humanity is thus divisive and to be rejected.

Indeed, how could anything be right or wrong, true or false in terms of truth status in any constant and abiding sense, since such terms indicating differentiation (right/wrong, good/evil, male/female, etc.,) are simply labels for different items throughout the advance (process) of psychological, biological and social evolution? All ostensibly absolute distinctions are either illusory, less than fully-real, or mere social conventions hardened into 'truth' in the interest of power for a given class in society. Naturally then, all religions, cultures, sexual practices, gender expressions or lifestyle choices are equally valid. Without this equality, the utopian holds, there can be no unity. Given the idea that all people are 'fragments of god,' no fragment can be more ultimate than another; all things must be levelled, for there must be unity in the godhead. Moreover, since all values are really just social constructs (what Hegel called 'objectivization') in a historical process where all things are becoming one (unity), all basic distinctions in created reality must necessarily be broken down. To draw down this belief from the abstract and land it in the concrete realm of present social engineering and political utopianism in North America, we need only point to the 'queering' of all things as the new social reality. Today, all over the U.S. and Canada (and most of Western Europe) our politicians, having bought into international utopianism, are co-operating for the redefinition of marriage, sexuality, family and even gender. It is not only that the sexual, social, cultural, historical and innate norms of heterosexual masculinity and femininity are being condemned as heterosexism, transphobia and homophobia, it is that the very idea that there are two genders is being denied. The obvious biological and corresponding social realities entailed in the terms 'male' and 'female' are increasingly no longer being viewed as normative in education, law, politics or even medicine.[33]

Politically, this 'unification' in the name of 'love' and care, is extending right into the dressing room and washroom where your children prepare for sports. Increasingly, one can express whatever gender one feels, irrespective of biology, and these distortions are protected by force of law. We are told that there are now many gender identities and sexual orientations. There are the transgendered, the 'two-spirited' (a Native American pagan concept for having both genders inside you), cross-dressers, gender-queers, the gender non-conforming and the androgynous. These people in turn may be Asexual, Bisexual, Lesbian, Gay, Transsexual and queer – it is difficult to keep up with the litany of new gender-identities and sexual practices being promoted by contemporary utopians. To oppose the promulgation of these identities or to offer care and counseling to those who wish to move away from such practices is an increasingly risky thing to do.

In the 2017 revision to the Canadian Criminal Code sections listing identifiable groups (which already included sexual orientation), the highly controversial ideological concepts generated by radical critical theory – *gender identity and expression* – were added to the identifiable groups listed in section 318(4) (this list also applies to section 319 – see 319(7)) and to section 718.2(a) (aggravating factors for sentencing) of the *Criminal Code*. The promoting and inciting of 'hatred' towards these newly created groups now includes making statements in a public place or making statements in any other setting than that of a private conversation. Although religious arguments are ostensibly considered a possible defense if they are made in 'good faith,' the subjectivity of both 'hatred' and 'good faith' give courts incredible latitude in finding someone guilty. In the event of a conviction, the offense carries up to two years in prison. Worse, a new Act to amend the Canadian Criminal Code targeting what has been dubbed 'conversion therapy,' (Bill C-4) states clearly in its preamble: "conversion therapy…is based on and propagates *myths and stereotypes* about sexual orientation and gender identity, including the myth that a person's sexual orientation and gender identity can and ought to be changed." Clearly here, biblical truth (cf. 1 Cor. 6:9-11) concerning human sexuality is condemned as myth and Christ's call to repentance from sexual sin is overtly rejected. Justice Minister David Lametti explained his rationale for the ban, saying: "Conversion therapy is premised on a lie, that being homosexual, lesbian, bisexual or trans is wrong and in need of fixing. Not only is that false, it sends a demeaning and a degrading message that undermines the dignity of individuals." So, on the authority of Mr. Lametti, God's Word, the authority of Christ, the teaching of the universal church and centuries of normative understandings of the human person are dismissed as lies to be overthrown, with resisters potentially cast into prison. With the seriousness of this threat in mind, it would be important to know how 'conversion therapy' is actually being defined. The Bill's definition is as follows:

> Conversion therapy means a practice, treatment or service designed to change a person's sexual orientation to heterosexual or gender identity to cisgender, or to repress or reduce non-heterosexual attraction or sexual behaviour.[34]

The language of the Bill already presupposes the validity of fictive ideological concepts in queer theory by using terms like 'cisgender' for the biological binary norm of male and female. André Schutten, Director of Law and Policy and General Legal Counsel for ARPA Canada, has recently warned pastors in Canada that:

> This bill, if passed as written, would make it a *criminal offence* to help a person struggling with their sexual orientation (e.g. a same-sex attracted Christian) or sexual thoughts or behaviour (e.g. watching gay porn) or gender identity (e.g. believe they are a man trapped inside a female body) to bring their thoughts, words, and deeds into conformity with the Word of God. But the pastor or counsellor would be free to encourage a man to explore same-sex desires or experiment with same-sex behaviour. Similarly, encouraging a teen girl to love and appreciate and care for the female body God designed and paired with her soul would be a criminal act. But the opposite (encouraging or experimenting with change from cisgender to genderqueer, nonbinary, transgender, etc.,) is permitted.[35]

Aside from the massive philosophical and theological implications of laws which deny the normative concept of a stable, established human nature – a reality that has always informed our civilization and all sane social orders – the immediate practical fallout means the steady collapse of human society at almost every level, including biological males using girls' changing rooms, competing as female athletes and being sent to female prisons. As Michael Brown summarizes it, "say goodbye to male and female, to masculinity and femininity, to 'biological sex' and say hello to genderqueer, gender non-conforming, transgender, and transsexual...if the categories of male and female are up for grabs in kindergarten, can you imagine what's coming next?"[36] To recognize, accept and celebrate these ideas as the highest social values is called 'love.' And to insist that all others recognize and celebrate them, and to require them as a matter of legislation and coercion, is 'justice.'

Therefore, by eliminating distinctions in gender, economic prosperity, ethnicity, knowledge, health, moral values and more, all mankind will be humanized, equalized and socialized, united as one universal entity and the unification of the godhead will have been achieved. At this dreamed-of historical moment, socialized humanity will finally be classless, stateless, family-less, gender-less, lawless, religion-less and an essentially structure-less collectivity of beings in harmony with themselves and the other (nature). The imagined equality here is both ontological (in terms of our being) and political. This love and unity, the progressive accomplishment of total social justice, is thus the great imperative of the utopian. We see this particularly in the 'repressive tolerance' agenda of Herbert Marcuse that has become the new orthodoxy throughout much of Western higher education. Those who oppose this woke vision, thereby hindering the realization of 'love' and 'unity,' are to be condemned as phobic, haters, heretics, disturbers of the peace and purveyors of the new atheism – belief in the God of the Bible. Such a view of reality based on a personal, relational God who transcends time and creation, who differentiates, judges, makes covenant, commands, and calls to repentance, cannot be tolerated as he destroys the unity of the new godhead. The heretics must be marginalized, silenced, imprisoned or cast out. This absolute requirement for the unity (oneness) of humanity as the essence of social justice or equity is the fundamental principle of the dystopian nightmare.

The Omnipotence of the Utopian Godhead

A second necessary aspect to any doctrine of God is *omnipotence*. Clearly, if God is not sovereign and all-powerful He cannot be God. Consequently, if sinful man's humanistic project is 'to be as God,' then as the new source of power, certainty and meaning, he must be omnipotent. Man as the new god must ape and *acquire* the characteristics of the living God in order to realize divinity. In order to be all-powerful, the new god, of necessity, must eliminate chance, impotence (powerlessness) and uncertainty from human affairs and this requires total control and omni-competence. We have already seen that utopians believe this will ultimately require a form of world-state with universal jurisdiction. It is only in terms of this theology of state that we can understand the aspirations of the United Nations with its ultimate goal of a global order, manifest in the proliferation of a litany of international bodies, institutions and treaties, from banks, to courts, to armies, lawmakers, agreements and cultural organizations for planning humanity's 'free' future when we will all be one.

The irony of this *coercive* pursuit of freedom through unity should not go unnoticed. Utopian power and control require the political use of coercion with the state functioning as 'man enlarged,' being the ultimate source of law and sovereign authority. It further requires the manipulation of nature in terms of organizational 'science' to eliminate uncertainty and demonstrate this omni-competence. Such a vision is obviously dystopian since it requires totalitarianism. This is not simply a technique for domination, it is a religious principle. Molnar observes: "It is a doctrinal necessity inscribed in Marxist theory. Totalitarianism prescribes total domination over man – over all his mental, spiritual, creative and technical endeavors, and its organization of these activities is the *sine qua non* of restoring man to a direct relationship with nature."[37] Total power is then an essential requirement to bring about the new utopia which mankind is said to both need and be destined for. Even if most people don't understand this destiny, the new philosopher kings, the elite social planners, believe they understand, and more importantly, know what is best for the rest of us.

To understand the reason for this we must note again an aspect of Marxist theory. In this worldview, the ideal world (from which man is alienated), is the *material* world (nature) reflected in the human mind and translated into thought forms. Human thought is then reduced, by radical reductionism, to rank materialism. As a consequence, true philosophy is not the love of wisdom, man reflecting carefully on human experience, both internal and external. It is rather 'work' or '*practice*' of the human sciences (total praxis). In other words, the concern of utopian thought is not with *describing* or explaining the inner and outer world, but with changing and *controlling* them. Since the human person is a part of the material of nature (all that is) and the progress of cosmic evolution, man is equally the legitimate object of scientific and social experiment. A totalitarian world of total control, of the science of organization and experimentation, thus replaces Christian theology and philosophy.

Whether the utopian delusion is expressed as a form of Marxism, neo-Marxism, National Socialism (Fascism), Fabian Socialism or some other political permutation, *power* is the central theme. Both Marxism and Fascism are totalitarian ideologies; one centred in class warfare where people are divided up into oppressor and oppressed groups, the other in elitism in which the superior must crush the inferior and weak. One calls for the *dictatorship* of the proletariat or the common wage laborer, the other for the *dictatorship* of the supermen. Both are instruments of naked power for the creation of a utopian society where, one way or another, man is becoming a god. In the twentieth century, both resulted in the expression of naked power involving brutal and horrific slaughter on an unprecedented scale. Both engaged in repression, torture, mass murder and 'scientific' experimentation on human individuals, families, communities and whole nations. Whether through the SS and Gestapo, or by officials of The Party, both sought total control of all aspects of the social order to create their brave new worlds. In both contexts, dissent could not be tolerated. Likewise both regimes claimed to act on behalf of nature (materialistic evolution), advancing mankind toward its destiny in godhood.

The true and living God remains the main obstacle to man's lust for total power and the creation of his dystopian nightmare. Once the idea of the God of the Bible is eliminated the stage of freedom from God or the stage of 'necessity' has been reached. In this stage of necessity, *nature and history dictate all human decisions and actions* with a total authority surpassing that of God himself. These dictates of nature cannot be refused. Molnar explains why: "First, because these dictates are proclaimed in the name of nature; secondly, because man is himself part of nature and of history, nothing remains in reference to which he might say 'no.'"[38] If nature and impersonal processes of history dictate human actions (historicism), then there is no transcendent appeal possible for man, no higher authority to which he may appeal against tyranny and slavery. The new order of unity and salvation is then the scientific, socialist state.

The 'One' (nature/god) is totally immanent and so there is no escape from the 'incarnate' truth. It becomes logical then that to resist this truth is not only backward, but evil. Man is thus absorbed into a *process* that is both necessary and irresistible. Accordingly, total predestinating power is demanded and sought by the state in the name of man's freedom – freedom to be part of nature and its determinative historical progress. In a profound irony, true freedom becomes the renunciation of freedom. The desire for individual freedom is seen as a kind of childhood of mankind, whereas collectivist freedom is to grow up into the maturity of mankind's freedom to fulfil his destiny. In such a view only the immanent divinity concept (nature manifest in statist man), not the transcendent God, can be allowed in human politics, since a God who is different from nature and claims power for himself, would always attract loyalty away from the one immanent god. With man as the only god, complete cohesion and unification is thought to be within reach.

Posthuman Omnipotence

So how might this vision of total power be realized in the real world? How might total control, total predestination – the necessary precursor to utopia – be achieved by man? One recent proposal pushes the belief in man's technology, scientific planning and providence to new heights. In the book, *The Last Prophet* by Haldane, communication by telepathy results in the emergence of a super-organism. The social consensus of humanity is conveyed by electronic waves automatically so that all community units (people) act in the common interest at all times. A similar idea is vividly expressed in the science fiction of *Star Trek,* especially in the feature film, *First Contact,* in which the Enterprise's heroic crew engages in a struggle for the survival of humanity against a collective consciousness called the *Borg.*

The Borg's goal is perfection, by the assimilation of all peoples and worlds into the Borg collective. The Borg, a race of part-organic, part-cybernetic automatons, are all interconnected by carrier waves so that there are effectively no individuals, or at least no individual wills, although there are millions of humanoid beings (drones). The Borg's claim in confronting races for assimilation is that their power is irresistible. All will be assimilated and 'resistance is futile.'

Granted, this is the realm of science fiction, yet such dreams of a new type of enhanced hybrid human actuate many scientists, technocrats and bureaucrats today – although the dream of man becoming a superman goes all the way back to the ancient pagan world. Surprising as it may sound, increasing numbers of ethicists, futurists and scientists hold that man can become a great deal more than he presently is by the use of emerging technologies that would include cognitive enhancement, behaviour modification, bionic implants and more. It is thought that these things may lead even to the defeat of death and mortality. Julian Huxley (1887-1975) first coined the term transhumanism in 1957. He claimed, "the human species can, if it wishes transcend itself – not just sporadically, an individual here in one way, an individual there in another way, but in its entirety, as humanity."[39] There are many current efforts underway to develop these ideas and move toward the reality of a 'transhuman' or posthuman world. James A. Herrick notes, "hundreds and perhaps thousands of university and corporate research facilities around the world are involved in developing artificial intelligence, regenerative medicine, life-extension strategies, and pharmaceutical enhancements of cognitive performance."[40] The goal is nothing short of self-salvation. As the Humanist Manifesto II makes clear, "no deity will save us; we must save ourselves."[41] Inspired in some measure by Nietzsche's 'Overman' (which glorified self-actualization), transhumanism (influenced by

Gnosticism, rationalism, science fiction and developed in the thinking of British philosopher Max More) has become a global intellectual and cultural movement with a considerable following amongst the intelligentsia.

Built on the cultural myths of particles to people evolution, progress, the superman and the power of a collective intellect, the eugenic idea has returned emphatically in transhumanism, but with a difference. The eugenics movement of the twentieth century, exemplified by the Nazi utopians, held that progress in evolution cannot now be achieved accidentally, with natural selection left to take its course, but must be controlled by deliberate selection, since intelligent man has become the custodian of evolution. The posthuman believers agree with this thesis, but realize that the old eugenics breeding program was scientifically flawed; in terms of genetics we are not inevitably 'improving,' since genetic entropy (the progressive accumulation of harmful mutations) is working in the other direction. Accordingly, for the transhumanists, *enhancement evolution* is the clear next step. Evolution, it is held, has produced us, and through us it has produced technology so that we are at the point where we can transform our own species by technological manipulation. The essential hope is that it will soon be possible to so integrate human technology (nanotechnology, biotechnology, information technology and cognitive science) with our natural physical, biological systems, that an effectively new species of man will arise that blends the technological and synthetic with the organic; man and machine merge into the transhuman.

This integration project begins with mechanically augmenting the body, but they believe it will end in an ability to deposit essential human consciousness in mechanical, artificial devices. This gradual transformation would include the extensive use of pharmaceuticals to enhance or alter cognitive functions and would be combined with an emphasis on re-education of the population about human nature. As computer scientist Hugo de Garis has put it, "because of our intelligence that's evolved over billions of years, we are now on the point of making a major transition away from biology to a new step. You could argue that...maybe humanity is just a stepping stone."[42] What was previously considered magic and mysticism in ancient paganism will now be pursued by technological means. Today, genetic manipulation is very much a reality, nanotechnology is advancing and human DNA is being looked at as a possible information storage device whilst many techno-futurists genuinely believe that within a generation human beings may be able to interact directly with cyberspace by immediate access via the cerebral cortex. Furthermore, some computer engineers reckon that our rate of progress will result in an Internet that is a trillion times faster than today's within forty years.[43] Not only is the emergence of the transhuman thought to be in the interests of enhancing human experience in progress toward something other, it is also reckoned to be humanity's only escape from extinction. Herrick writes:

> Professor Julian Savulescu is the head of the Uehiro Centre for Practical Ethics at Oxford University and a leading proponent of human enhancement, the school of thought that promotes the progressive use of biotechnologies to improve human intellect, moral reasoning, and other traits such as physical strength. Savulescu has argued that deep moral flaws and destructive behaviors point indisputably to the need to employ technology and education to change human nature; either we take this path or we face extinction as a species...according to Savulescu, genetic science, improved pharmaceuticals, and moral education may hasten the emergence of a new and better human race.[44]

Such men genuinely believe that technology will conquer everything from outer space to death itself; human nature will thus be conquered, delivering humanity into the future as evolved demigods. Interestingly, in this process, the Internet is viewed as man's first great step toward a unified consciousness.[45] This vague idea of a unified consciousness is expressed in Teilhard de Chardin's "noosphere," in Ray Kurzweil's "singularity," and in Bertrand Russell's, "world of shining beauty and transcendent glory" that will blanket the earth and pervade the universe.[46] This 'omega point' is a globally integrated, immortal race.

The pagan, religious nature of these ideas, though shrouded in the language of 'science,' is very clear. The ultimate goal is not simply the emergence of a bionic man with an interconnected consciousness through cyberspace. The basic belief is that evolution, or the universe itself (the process of nature) through its human and then posthuman offspring and their technological innovation, is moving toward complete omniscience and *omnipotence*. "Ambitious evolution is merely using us and our descendants as its cat's paw to snatch technological divinity from the cosmos's chaotic flames."[47] Kurzweil has stated clearly, "the universe will wake up; it will become intelligent and that will multiply our intelligence trillions upon trillions...; it is called the Singularity. But regardless what you call it, it will be the universe waking up. Does God exist? I would say, 'not yet.'[48] This faith is therefore a religious trust in the posthuman potential, a radical humanism that is fervently committed to the belief that man can transform his humanity to godhood, seizing the attributes of God and achieving immortality, universal knowledge, and unified global consciousness."[49] This faith is also an *organized* religion. As David Herbert has pointed out in his book-length study of Transhumanism, "Singularity University (SU) was the brainchild of Peter Diamandis (b. 1961), physician and noted entrepreneur. The inspiration for this venture came about after reading *The Singularity is Near*. Soon after, Dr Diamandis successfully enlisted Ray Kurzweil, the author of the book, to join him in creating this unique educational institution." Their goal is disruptive thinking and creative solutions that solve the planet's most pressing challenges.[50] Kurzweil was made the university's first chancellor.

Now there is a necessary link between the goal of man transcending his humanity and the need for increased limitations on human freedoms – including freedom of speech and religion, the right of privacy and the erosion of free sovereign nations through the *seizure of power* by a global authority. In essence, to acquire power over nature (that is, himself), man will need total power over people. As Herrick explains, for Savulescu, "more is needed, including worldwide cooperation 'in a way that humans have never so far cooperated.'"[51] Once again global government and control is apparently necessary for man to reach his divine potential. According to some posthuman experts, "the near future will usher in a global culture enabled by a massively more powerful Internet…." Hugo de Garis takes as simple matters of fact that "technical progress will create within forty years…a global media, a global education system, a global language, and a globally homogenized culture," which will constitute the basis of "a global democratic state."[52] This massive centralization of power for the common good will of course require us all to surrender our historic commitment to freedom. Savulescu writes:

> We could reduce our commitment to liberalism. We will, I believe, need to relax our commitment to maximum protection of privacy. We're already seeing an increase in the surveillance of individuals, and that surveillance will be necessary if we're to avert the threats that those with anti-social personality disorders, psychopathic personality disorders, or fanaticism represent through their access to radically enhanced technology.[53]

Total power means total surveillance and the elimination of privacy in order to neutralize the threat from those who have *anti-social personality disorders* or who are *fanatics*. Contemporary utopianism already identifies those who oppose the legalization and promotion of the queering of culture as 'mentally ill' individuals suffering from irrational phobias, and the fanatics are of course the traditional religionists, the Christians: "Traditional religion has been the *bête noir* of enhancement advocates, an anti-technological and anti-futurist force to be actively opposed."[54] Transhumanism is clearly a religious utopianism growing in strength and influence with a real faith in the singularity – the One. Here we meet not only the lust for total power, but once again the pursuit of unity in the godhead which requires the use of power to reach this end. The common creed, motivating a delusional craving for total predestinating power is that "ongoing evolution will 'eventually produce a unified cooperative organization of living processes that spans and manages the universe as a whole."[55] But since the leading transhumanists (aspiring bureaucrats for the universe), like everyone else, are being overtaken by death, what can be done to save them for the singularity? Herbert tells us:

> Kurzweil has set in motion an alternate plan – cryonics. He has already made arrangements with the Alcor Life Extension Foundation to have his body cryopreserved…. Even though we do not presently have the means of reviving bodies cryonically preserved, technology, as always, will be the panacea to gain eternal life – and thus we 'will be like God.'[56]

If ever there were a working manifestation of the demonic urge 'to be as god,' this is certainly it – a cosmos-sized unified bureaucracy of 'living processes' inclusive of the technologically resurrected, managing the entire universe through the emergence of a cosmic mind, a counterfeit god.

It may seem far-fetched that men are seeking the *power* to alter the very essence of human nature into a grotesque hybrid of semi-cybernetic life, followed by assimilation into some form of universal collective, but this is the utopianism of humanism. Decades before today's futurists, H. G. Wells, a utopian *par excellence*, spoke of the 'process of thought' of which all are a part, growing in range and power without limit! Wells believed man as a collective could be immortal.[57] In this quest, man's task is to subordinate himself to the 'immortal being of the race' – all are to give themselves to that which increases knowledge and power.[58] To the ensuring of this end there should be no delay. Wells writes, "My idea of politics is an open conspiracy to hurry these tiresome, wasteful, evil things – nationality and war – out of existence; to end this empire and that empire, and set up the one Empire of Man."[59] This will come about when man gives himself to the collective and to science. 'We can all be citizens of the free state of science.'

The impediment to accomplishing this glorious 'state of science' as Wells saw it was people's feebleminded attachment to God. "[O]ur political, our economic, our social lives which have still to become illuminated and directed by the scientific spirit, are still sick and feeble with congenital traditionalism."[60] What is the solution? "A great release of human energy and a rapid dissolution of social classes, through the ever-increasing efficiency of economic organization and the utilization of mechanical power."[61] In other words, man's transcendental aspiration, to 'grow in range and power without limit,' require coercive political power to dissolve the classes and the use of technology, or scientific control. For the most part, contemporary Western intellectuals (especially the new left) believe power must be used to demolish the traditional family, the orthodox Christian faith and any hint of social classes – only then can the necessary economic transformation take place to advance the collectivist cause.

This Dagon of neo-Marxist technocracy has come into sharp focus in the early 2020s as various globalist and transnational organisations have promoted their vision for the emergence of a technocratic global order and fourth industrial revolution in the wake of Covid-19. Klaus Schwab, the founder of one such globalist organisation – the highly influential World Economic Forum – published a book in 2020 called Covid-19: The Great Reset. Using the novel virus as a pretext for increased global controls on every aspect of life, he bemoans the failure of global governance and leadership in allowing social divides and an absence of cooperation. The time is now, he claims, for a new world order to emerge, the contours of which we can imagine and draw for ourselves. Things will never go back to normal, because the globalists have a new normal in mind for us. "Many of our beliefs and assumptions about what the world could or should look like will be shattered in the process." The unprecedented lockdowns of human society in various nations were embraced with a kind of sumptuous glee by elites sharing Schwab's desire for a technocratic global revolution.

Using familiar euphemisms for global technocracy, Schwab celebrates the massive consolidation of power in 'government' and its intervention in every department of life throughout his book, all in the name of pursuing 'global public goods' such as health and climate change solutions. The 'global contours' that he sees emerging from the crisis are transparently neo-Marxist ambitions that skew reality and mispresent the Protestant heritage of the West, in particular the UK and United States:

> [T]he post-pandemic era will usher in a period of massive wealth redistribution, from the rich to the poor and from capital to labour. Second, Covid-19 is likely to sound the death knell of neoliberalism, a corpus of ideas and policies that can loosely be defined as favoring competition over solidarity, creative

destruction over government intervention and economic growth over social welfare ... these two concomitant forces – massive redistribution on the one hand and abandoning neoliberal policies on the other – will exert a defining impact on society's organization, ranging from how inequalities could spur social unrest to the increasing role of governments and the redefinition of social contracts.[62]

The key to the new world is therefore technocracy – not just the utilization of new technologies, but mankind embracing the ideas of new elite group of planners. 'Will we get our global house in order' is the great question for Schwab – which is the essence of the so-called Great Reset. The obstacle is nationalism of course, which Schwab bemoans as a world in which nobody is really in charge: "global governance and international cooperation are so intertwined that it is nigh on impossible for global governance to flourish in a divided world." There is no progress possible for Schwab without 'shared intentionality' manifest in all peoples striving together toward a common goal. What is that common goal? It is to address and ultimately eliminate the perceived existential threats to Mother Nature, which for Schwab are fourfold: nuclear threats, climate change, unsustainable resource use and inequalities between peoples. Planetary salvation thus depends on technocratic globalism.

The wielding of this total power to bring about a utopian order, with or without the dream of the posthuman cyborg, requires a vast nanny state bureaucracy by which the whole of life is managed. The transition to Utopia may be traumatic, we are told, but it is for the best. Gradually, various societal instruments of freedom and power are withdrawn from individuals and families so that power is concentrated in the source of divinity – the power state. Private property and ownership is one of the first such freedoms to be targeted. Progressive taxation of income, property, inheritance and now even carbon, leads to open and brazen assaults on private property, including direct seizure of money from bank accounts and of land or goods.[63] Money, a form of private property whereby one form of property is converted into another, is therefore a means of power or dominion. Private property must be steadily abolished because it introduces a rival power or source of resistance to the power-state. Wealth and property must be equalized and become 'collective property,' owned by the state and a small group of elites. All men then become children, dependent upon public assistance.[64] The most powerful social entity then owns and completely controls the source of power. A moment's reflection reveals that today, the modern utopian is a good way toward realizing such goals:

> The fact is, that the concept of the state (or the community), completely dominating and regulating the lives of its citizens, has been, by and large, accepted in the second half of the twentieth century...the debate of the past several decades has been merely whether the state, the race, the ideological empire or World Government will stage-manage the last acts of the passage to a coalescing mankind.[65]

The utopian evidently sees nature as a source of unlimited power. If that power can only be properly harnessed, all the potentiality of man can be focused on the conquest of other planets, solar systems, death and all laws and norms transcending man himself. The ultimate goal is therefore the acquisition of complete power over life, things and people; in essence, it is the will to be God.

The delusions of men in this regard are staggering. The scientific socialist future was the one that Orwell contemplated with horror. Science in this vision becomes only what serves man's purpose – which, as we have seen, is power and control as an end. Society itself becomes an experiment and an exercise in material manipulation. For any experiment to be valid, the basic requirement is total control of the environment – all the factors must be under controlled conditions. Therefore, in the utopian vision of society as a social experiment, a totalitarian vision is a necessary starting point, without which the experiment will be neither valid nor scientific. This is what is said with regard to the failures of Marxism in its political regimes past and present – there was or is a failure to foresee or control certain factors. Having learnt from these mistakes, many in the intelligentsia believe the experiment can now function properly – unforeseen variables can be eliminated. No longer about understanding reality, science has become the task of controlling it.

So rather than the Christian view of reality, which leaves predestination to God – thereby leaving man in a place of liberty by denying the right of total control to any human agency – the scientific society believes its desired social results can be obtained by means of controlled causation. This has led scientists, futurists and political utopians to discuss or pursue everything from cloning to the modification of human organs, the creation of a synthetic human being, control of the weather, elimination of crime by treatment, modification of food, colonization of the universe, development of an artificial sun, elimination of disease, creation of transhumans, forced sterilization, and postponement or deliverance from death.[66] This new tower of Babel seems terrifying and imposing, as intimidating as the great statue of Nebuchadnezzar doubtless appeared to the prophet Daniel and his friends, but the Christian must not, indeed cannot fear, nor can we yield because "The world of the future shall be God's world, and man in that world shall be only what the predestinating power and control of God intend him to be."[67]

The Wrath of Man

One further logical development of man's dystopian will to *power* is the arrogation to himself of the power to judge and pour out wrath as the new god; in a world rejecting the living

God, the need for judgement has not vanished. If God's covenantal judgements in history are denied, man's word of blessing and cursing must replace them. If God's transcendent court and judgement are abolished in man's thinking, then man needs to create for himself a purely world-bound and temporal court for absolute judgement, and consign men to an immanent hell for disobedience. If history is all there is, judgement cannot be delayed. To delay judgement is to hinder progress toward Oneness and unity. As Albert Camus put it, "the judgement pronounced by history must be pronounced immediately, for culpability coincides with the check to progress and with punishment."[68]

The Christian view of reality can give men maximum freedom under the law and need not insist on absolute and immediate judgement in history over all sin, because ultimate judgement and the judgement of men's hearts and motives belongs to God alone. Without the living God, however, the utopian state fills the vacuum in man's craving for judgement. The terror involved in such a view is that this de-facto god, the power state, has no transcendent critique since there is *no God in judgement over it.* The utopian recognizes that not all the population will agree with his vision of a total order that doles out summary judgement against the structural oppressors[69] and resisters, so in political discourse the 'people' or the 'real' population are the abstract group upon which the new unanimity is established. This public is then indoctrinated to internalize the (politically) correct way of thinking while the non-conformers are punished with a loss of social credit for their bigotry, intolerance, rejection of the democratic will, sexism, classism, nationalism, heterosexism and a variety of psychological phobias that multiply by the week. To the scientific planners the utopian worldview is allegedly so self-evident that only the perverted would resist it and must be put on trial, by media, politics or tribunal, for their violation of the new positive human rights – this is the presently tame expression of temporal judgement in the West. The brutal interference of the state in the Chinese 'commune' system is well-documented (including the regulation of the sex lives of married couples), and yet these horrors give Western intellectuals little pause. Molnar comes to the disturbing crux of the matter:

> All this is done in order to change the nature of man, extirpate his selfishness and instill collective conscience…. The Utopian leadership always claims that its function is merely to facilitate association among equal citizens, including among members of a family – or in the religious utopian language, communication between them and God. Under such a claim the citizen shows his virtuousness to the extent that he abandons the socially divisive attitude of looking out for his own and his family's interests, and with a complete loyal candor, trusts the leadership class to take care of his needs…conversely, doubt in, and resistance to, this ability (and love) show stupidity, obstinacy and viciousness: doubters and resisters must be punished… since they contradict the associative principle and break unanimity, doubters and resisters must first be excluded from the membership of utopia's citizenry, hence from membership in the human race. The utopian who has scorned and abolished the coercive power of the state, with its police, laws, courts and executioners, proceeds to restore them in the most matter of fact way…on the extermination of resisters to utopia all utopian writers are in agreement.[70]

Nations Under God

Earlier in the chapter I argued that a biblical view of mankind and of the state can never produce the utopian idealism that we are witnessing today, and indeed have witnessed in different guises throughout history. The receptivity of many Christians to utopian ideas is in part due to their aping of the Christian message as well as the various ways the core utopian doctrines are disguised in euphemisms. Critically, the phrase *du jour* that is being used to express the contemporary utopian program is globalism. We can recognize its ideological nature by the *-ism* suffix, which is usually an indicator that some *aspect* of life is being abstracted and depicted as its absolute essence. Utopian globalism sees the technological developments and change described above not simply as enhancing international relations but heralding a new era that will certainly lead to the decline of separate states. It puts religious hope in the promise of a democratized, technocratic world beyond war and poverty with universal rights emerging from a pagan/secular worldview. The ultimate goal of globalism is the subsuming of cultures, states and economies within one global international law-order (including supra-national government) with each of us living as world citizens. As such, globalism is the epitome of utopianism, its adherents regarding it as an historical necessity – i.e., globalism is inevitable, and we cannot turn back.

The Genetics of Globalism

To understand today's globalism – often going under other expressions like transnationalism, new world order, global governance, right side of history etc., – it is important to go back to Scripture for an understanding of this vision for human society. In the West, two visions of the world's political life have battled against each other for centuries. One posits independent sovereign nations/states pursuing political life in terms of their own customs and traditions. The other sees the world united under a single political law-order, maintained by a supranational authority.

The first view, which we will call biblical nationalism, can be traced back to the Older Testament and the establishment of the nation of Israel. When God first calls Abraham and tells him that he is going to make a great nation of him and bless all the families of the earth through this new people, no empire over the earth is offered to Abraham (Gen 12:1-3). Such a thing is never offered to Israel's patriarchs, kings or rulers. We will return later to the reason for that in the universal reign of Jesus Christ – the root of redeemed humanity. But it is immediately noteworthy that Scripture itself offers an alternate picture to the utopian pagan vision that has dominated world history. God's idea was of an independent nation without imperial ambitions. That is, a number of tribes gathered together in a given and limited territory with a common religion, language and unique constitution.

Because of the Christian gospel and the presence of the Bible at the heart of Western civilization for centuries, a perpetual struggle has gone on between the pagan globalist dream and the scriptural vision of independent nations which look back to the constitution of Israel. For example, with the Reformation and a return to Scripture, nation states like England and the Netherlands broke with the authority of the Holy Roman Empire, leading to four centuries of Protestant nation-building in Western Europe and America. In these lands, national sovereignty and self-determination were regarded as foundational principles basic to true social and political freedom.

The second vision is obviously utopian imperialism, which, updated to common parlance, we can call globalism. This view originates with the Tower of Babel and the numerous pagan imperial powers which followed (Gen. 10:8-12; 11:1-9). There was a succession of imperial powers seeking empire: Egypt, Babylonia, Assyria, Persia, Greece and of course the Roman Empire. Later there was an attempted synthesis of the pagan view with Christianity in the West under the Holy Roman Empire. Other essentially pre-modern attempts at world empire were made by the Mongol Empire founded by Genghis Khan and the Islamic Ottoman Empire (which only ended with World

War I). The European colonial powers of the modern era had a religiously distinctive character to the notions of world empire originating in the premodern world, especially the British Commonwealth of independent nations that emerged from the British Empire. However, even the British Empire was infected with some elements of the same virus of utopian imperialism, just as the United States after World War II (particularly with the re-formation of the League of Nations as the United Nations and its growing influence at the end of the Cold War) increasingly pursued a global regime of international law to be imposed on all nations.

As Britain and America began secularising and drifting from scriptural foundations, the faulty presumption was made that inherited ideas such as constitutional democracy, republicanism, the rule of law and individual liberties should be immediately understood and desired by everyone, which failed to take seriously that such ideas and practices are the cultural inheritance of certain tribes and nations emerging from specific religious beliefs over many centuries. Today, Western empire-building has re-emerged with the liberal-imperialist notion of globalism. The proponents of this view share a clearly defined imperialist perspective in which the secular liberal vision of society, enshrined in its radical equalitarian and egalitarian principles for planetary salvation are codified as universal law and imposed upon the nations by transnational institutions, treaties and bodies, if necessary by force.

The seeds of modern globalism were planted in the Enlightenment era as cultural elites began turning away from Christianity and the vision of the Protestant nation state and started formulating globalist manifestos, emulating the ancient Greeks. For Plato and Aristotle all sociological questions concerned the theory of the *polis* – an all-encompassing religious and political community which envisioned no areas of life outside the state's total control. In Immanuel Kant's *Perpetual Peace: A Philosophical Sketch* (1795) he attacked the idea of the national state as a form of barbarism and in the name of reason called for an international state over all the earth under a universal law. He writes:

> There is only one rational way in which states co-existing with other states can emerge from the lawless condition of pure warfare … they must renounce their savage and lawless freedom, adapt themselves to public coercive laws, and thus form an international state which would necessarily grow until it embraced all the people of the earth.[71]

This was for Kant the dictate of reason and to oppose it was to resist the journey of humankind toward a universal reign of reason. Kant's basic premise is that a crooked human nature could be renovated and improved through governmental institutions and international law. The ultimate goal is achieving reasonableness in the individual and finally a world state. Variations on this basic idea became incredibly popular with the intellectual class in Western culture. A spiritualized form of it stemming from Hegel's thought sees the movement toward globalism as the unfolding of Spirit in history. The "world historical" individual (the leading society) moves the world toward the nebulous idea of absolute Spirit. This is accomplished not, as in biblical faith, at the consummation of Christ's kingdom, but at the point of human civilization's reunification with 'god' (world Spirit). On this view, globalism is a dialectical phase of the embodiment of 'god's' will unfolding on earth.

Again, revealing its utopian character, globalism requires conformity, through force if necessary. Rational (i.e. secular liberal) universal principles must be embodied everywhere for the well-being of all the earth; any principles, practices or institutions that cannot be embraced universally (i.e. biblical truth and institutions) must be transcended. Traditional religion (i.e. biblical faith) is divisive, not 'rational' and so cannot be universalized and provide a basis for a global society. Jewish philosopher Yoram Hazony has pointed out that:

> Under a universal political order ... tolerance for diverse political and religious standpoints must necessarily decline. Western elites whose views are now being aggressively homogenized in conformity with the new liberal construction, are finding it increasingly difficult to recognize a need for the kind of toleration of divergent standpoints that the principle of national self-determination had once rendered axiomatic. Tolerance, like nationalism, is becoming a relic of a bygone age ... the emerging liberal construction is incapable of respecting, much less celebrating, the deviation of nations seeking to assert a right to their own unique laws, traditions and policies. Any such dissent is held to be vulgar and ignorant, if not evidence of a fascistic mind-set ... campaigns of delegitimization, in both Europe and America, have been directed against the practice of Christianity and Judaism, religions on which the old biblical political order is based ... it requires [no special insight] to see that this is only the beginning, and that the teaching and practice of traditional forms of Judaism and Christianity will become ever more untenable as the liberal construction advances ... genuine diversity in the constitutional or religious character of the Western nations persists only at mounting cost to those who insist on their freedom.[72]

The Scriptural Response

The late nineteenth and early twentieth century philosopher of history, Oswald Spengler, embodies the radical humanistic mentality of the globalist when he claims that technology will place in human hands a world created by itself and obedient to itself – the diabolic seed of his thought is unmistakeable:

> A will to power, which mocks all bounds of time and space and makes the infinite and eternal its goal, subjects whole parts of the world to itself, finally embraces the whole globe with its communication and information technology, and transforms it

through the power of its practical energy and the awesomeness of its technological methods.[73]

It is difficult to see how such perverted ambition, embracing not only the globe itself but defying all time and space, could lead to anything but tyranny and dictatorship, abolishing freedom and crushing human flourishing. Such a globalist vision distorts the cultural mandate with human arrogance, hubris and rebellion.

We have seen that from a scriptural standpoint, the root of such ambitions is located in the spirit of Babel, where humanity in pretended autonomy opposes the Creator and his Law-Order for creation. The false religion of Babel – idealizing one unified humanity under a humanistic power-state operating in defiance of God to make all things subject to man's power and glory – is the original utopian delusion. In our time it ends up placing power and control in the hands of elites, banking cartels, multinational corporations and transnational powers and agencies. As such, a biblical resistance to globalism is a matter of preserving actual freedom for real national communities around the world, not simply a theoretical philosophical exercise.

Earlier I also noted that God did not give to the patriarchs, Moses or the kings of Israel a universal political mandate or imperial sanction to build empire. It is certainly true that God's Word is given to all people, the prophets were to speak God's law for the instruction of all the nations (Is. 42:4), and the seed of Abraham would be for the blessing of all peoples (Gen. 22:18). However, the nation of Israel itself was limited to prescribed borders and had no authority to impose by force its way of life on the nations around it. It was to be a model, a light and example, a prophetic voice, but not an imperial power.

Clearly, there was a missiological purpose for Israel as a nation-state (Deut. 4:5-8) as there is in God's providential ordination of the boundaries of the various nations of the world.

The apostle Paul made this clear to the pagan utopian thinkers in Athens:

> From one man He has made every nationality to live over the whole earth and has determined their appointed times and the boundaries of where they live. He did this so they might seek God, and perhaps they might reach out and find Him, though He is not far from each one of us (Acts 17:26-27).

This biblical view stands in stark contrast to that of the pagan nations of antiquity and of their modern globalist heirs. Hazony points out:

> This Mosaic view is diametrically opposed to that offered by Kant's supposed enlightened imperialism, which asserts that moral maturity arrives with the renunciation of national independence and the embrace of a single universal empire. But there is no moral maturity in the yearning for a benevolent empire to rule the earth and take care of us, judging for us and enforcing its judgements upon us. It is in fact nothing but a plea to return to the dependency of childhood ... true moral maturity is attained only when we stand on our own feet, learning to govern ourselves and defend ourselves without needlessly harming those around us, and where possible also extending assistance to neighbors and friends. And the same is true for nations, which reach genuine moral maturity when they can live in freedom and determine their own course, benefitting others where this is feasible, yet with no aspiration to impose their rule and their laws on other nations by force ... we should shoulder the burdens of national freedom and independence that we have received as an inheritance from our forefathers.[74]

As such, the genuinely Christian alternative to globalism is a scriptural form of nationhood that recognizes the true basis of unity in the human community in Christ and under His Word, not in man-imposed global political unification. Yet steeped as we have been in secular utopian assumptions for decades, this authentically Christian alternative is distasteful to many modern believers. Nonetheless, the other typical responses offered as alternatives by Christians are simply inadequate to resist the forceful march of liberal imperialism. The neo-Catholic approach – that has been frequently adopted by many evangelicals and two-kingdoms advocates in the Reformed camp – seeks to embrace a natural law theory of 'universal reason' indebted to the Stoics and Enlightenment philosophers rather than Scripture, in maintaining some sort of moral minimum for the functioning of the state. This ancient Greek idea of an eternal law of reason in which the mind of both God and man participates – thereby making natural law 'publicly accessible' in a way that biblical revelation supposedly does not – is inevitably susceptible and sympathetic to ideas of universal human rights deduced from human reason along with their enforcement by some form of international regime. Whilst such Christians frequently oppose abortion and usually support traditional ideas of marriage, they lack a clear basis on which to resist the growth of the state in controlling all areas of life and the globalist drive of modern progressivism.

Likewise, the 'contractarians' among Christians who see basic cohesion in society as built around loyalty to the state rather than religious commitment to Christ, tend to view the state as a neutral apparatus charged only with a vague notion of the 'common good' as defined by the social contract. It seems only logical that such a contract could span the nations of Europe (the European Union), and eventually, some sort of global order. Such Christians wish to distance the state from any fundamental obligation to scriptural standards or biblical moral traditions and in so doing offer passive support to both statism and globalism without necessarily championing it.

The truly Christian alternative to globalism, with its scripturally informed idea of nationhood under God, is well summarized by Hazony as a standpoint that seeks to defend an international order of nation-states based on two principles of

Protestant (Calvinistic) construction: 'national independence and the biblical moral minimum for legitimate government.' This he describes as 'the freest, and in many respects the most successful, international order that has ever existed.' He identifies the biblical heritage of the Anglo-American conservative tradition inherited from people like Edmund Burke as:

> A Nationalist political tradition that embraces the principles of limited executive power, individual liberties, public religion based on the bible, and a historical empiricism that has so often served to moderate political life in Britain and America in comparison with that of other countries.[75]

Since the biblical idea of a nation-state under God with public religion based on Scripture is not worked out in detail in the Bible into a systematic political philosophy, a Protestant (or Calvinist) construction was helpfully fleshed out by the Christian philosopher Herman Dooyeweerd in terms of a worldview applicable to modern human society under four basic beliefs:

> (1) All social institutions, whether past or present, find their ultimate origin in creation. In creation, all things were separated "after their own kind" and vested with the "right to exist" and develop.

> (2) God is the absolute sovereign over all creation, at its inception and in its unfolding ... His sovereignty is absolute and constant: no creature and no activity is ever exempt from His authority.

> (3) God's authority is a legal authority. He established creation and governs His creatures by law ... The laws of creation communicate the will of the Creator. They provide order and constancy, not chaos and indeterminacy. Because God's sovereignty is absolute and constant, His law is comprehensive and continually obligates all creatures in all their activities...

(4) Under the laws of creation, each social institution has a "legal right" to exist alongside other individuals and institutions. It also has a legal duty to function in accordance with God's creation ordinances and providential plan, to fulfil its task or calling in history...earthly sovereignty is subservient to the absolute sovereignty of God.[76]

These fundamental commitments imply that just as the family, church and state enjoy a God-given legal right to exist and function in their own sovereign spheres under God, guaranteeing their freedom from interference by other spheres, so also each nation has a right to exist under the sovereignty of God, and be free to serve Him. Since God's creation Word and inscripturated Word do not contradict each other, the purposes of God in establishing the nations and their boundaries as taught in the Bible and seen in God's creation norms for human society, are all for the advancement of His kingdom.

This also implies that the nations are *ultimately obligated by God to be Christian* (cf. Ps. 2; Ps. 110; Is. 42:1-6; Phil. 2). No one nation has the authority to impose God's Law-Word upon another nation, for the King of kings Himself, in whom is vested all authority in heaven and on earth, is building His kingdom in all the nations, through the gospel witness of His people in all of life. This principle clearly involves respecting the legitimate authority of other nations to exist, establish their own laws and follow their customs and traditions, without being coerced by more powerful nations or globalist bodies to bow before a planetary regime of international laws.

The rejection of globalism however, does not condemn humanity to perpetual conflict, war and disharmony. Globalism as utopian ideology reflects, in part, a deep religious hunger and urge toward the unity and peace of the human race. The problem is that it seeks to accomplish this in an idolatrous way, distorting the cultural mandate. The biblical vision is that all the nations, by the work and witness of the gospel, will find true unity despite their diversity in and through the Lord Jesus Christ. When humanity acts in terms of its own pretended autonomy and authority to build a global empire it robs human society of the liberating reality of true freedom, harmony and peace that can only be realized in and through the gospel of the kingdom. As Dooyeweerd wrote:

> The Christian religion, linked to the Old Testament revelation, provides a new religious ground-motive for reflection on the foundations of human society. It is the theme of creation, fall into sin, and redemption by Christ Jesus in the communion of the Holy Spirit. It reveals that the religious community of the human race is rooted in creation, in the solidarity of the Fall into sin, and in the spiritual kingdom of God through Christ Jesus (the Corpus Christi). In this belief Christianity destroys in principle any claim made by a temporal community to encompass all of human life in a totalitarian sense.[77]

The key to a sure future of justice and peace is committing our thought, lives and nations to the kingdom of God in Jesus Christ which has come and will come – for all the world is subject to that future by God's own determination. This is an eschatological future certainty, progressively manifest in history and reaching its consummation at the return of Christ – "for the earth shall be filled with the knowledge of the Lord's glory as the waters cover the sea" (Hab. 2:14). There in the New Jerusalem, the final state affirms a rich cultural diversity of languages, ethnicities and national identities, because the Word of God will have been applied and contextualized amongst every people of the earth:

> And they sang a new song: You are worthy to take the scroll and to open its seals, because You were slaughtered, and You redeemed people for God by Your blood from every tribe and language and people and nation. You made them a kingdom and priests to our God, and they will reign on the earth (Rev. 5:9-10).

Universal empire belongs to our High Priest and King, Jesus Christ alone.

Chapter 3

RELIGION, GOVERNMENT AND
THE SECULARIST ILLUSION

You Gotta Serve Somebody

We saw emerging in the foregoing chapter the beginnings of
a distinctly Christian view of nationhood and government and
we noticed that this distinctiveness is rooted in very different
basic beliefs to the dominant political perspective of modern
intellectuals and contemporary Western culture in general. I
also pointed out that these antithetical visions for human society
have ancient roots, undergirded by contrasting presuppositions.
This reveals that analysing a truly Christian view of government
must actually involve a careful consideration of the nature and
meaning of religion. If that makes us narrow our eyes, it's
probably because we have been conditioned to think for two or
three generations that religion is something belonging to a
private arena of life that can have no decisive bearing on the
public space. Even if you live in a country where church and
state are not completely separated (the United Kingdom for
example), modern Western governments still operate on the
assumption of an implicit separation between the 'personal
faith' of politicians and civil administrators and the values,
mission and responsibilities of government.

Moreover, we have been deeply steeped in a reductionistic
understanding of government that presumes the use of the

definite article. We speak of "the government" as though the administrators of civil life were the only ones involved in the business of governing – yet this truncation of government also has a religious character. The biblical worldview acknowledges the public legal order as just one of several legitimate, God-ordained spheres of authority (that is, governance), all of which are created to function in subjection to the authority of Jesus, the King of kings. So I begin this discussion reflecting on the nature and role of religion because, fundamentally, I believe the operative presupposition of a separation of faith and government, of religion and the public space is an impossible myth. It is a lie, used to push the Christian faith out of sight and mind, replacing it with a new religious order.

The question of government is really a question of true or false worship. In the words of the poet Bob Dylan, you gotta serve somebody...

The Need to Explain

Upon serious reflection it is evident that there is an unbreakable link between our concept of God (a divine or unconditioned reality), our view of ourselves, and how we choose to live in the world. Which is to say, what we believe shapes how we behave – our ideas have real-world consequences. This is because, from a scriptural standpoint, human beings are integral creatures and religious by nature. By integral I mean first that humankind is not formed of two or more alien substances, temporarily bound together (like soul substance and material substance as many ancient Greeks held) in an uncomfortable union, but are made whole as God's image-bearers and find that all the various aspects of our lives and experience come together in a concentration point we often call the heart, or soul – the inner person or religious root of our being (2 Cor. 4:16; 1 Pt. 3:4).

Second, it is in this heart that we long for harmony between the various aspects of life – we seek an integral life. Ordinarily we dislike contradiction and confusion. If we truly believe something and are committed to it, we typically want that fact to shape our thinking and living. We generally seek to avoid blatant inconsistency. We abhor hypocrisy (especially in others) and are driven by a desire for unity and integrity in our lives that results in a sense of overall purpose and meaning. In other words, we are wired to seek to integrate the various aspects of our lives into a coherent whole. If we don't do this our lives start to fall apart – to disintegrate.

We are also religious beings. This, I suggest, is an inescapable aspect of the human condition (Acts 17:22-23; Rom 1:18-25). There have been many attempts to explain human religious sensibility. Modernist philosophers have tried to account for the hardwired religious inclination of humanity in terms of the contrast between man and the magnitude of the cosmos he inhabits – a shoreless universe inspiring him with awe and fear. The various 'religions,' they claim, developed as a defense mechanism in which many unseen forces were posited, deified, sometimes anthropomorphized, and then ritually placated as a way of trying to gain some kind of control in a dangerous world, despite a sense of powerlessness. This is a typically secular and simplistic account of religion that implies modern technological man has outgrown such things; modern man now offers scientific explanations for various phenomena instead.

While there is an element of truth in seeing certain pagan religious practices as a form of defense mechanism, the ongoing prevalence of all kinds of superstitious beliefs about the world in our own culture undermines secular simplistic explanations. Just consider the West's huge contemporary interest in pagan religion, mythology and witchcraft, as well as the ubiquity of occultism, alternative medicine, spiritism, and astrology, and the incredible popularity of Eastern religions like Buddhism,

Hinduism, and what was dubbed in the 1970s the New Age (a term no longer used because it is now mainstream). The idea that our era has outgrown various divinity beliefs and concepts in the wake of the scientific revolution, or that empirical science has essentially dispensed with various 'spiritual' perspectives on the world is patently false. Humans are religious beings who cannot help but seek to refer themselves back to the origin of all things.

Life is Religion

It is admittedly notoriously difficult to define religion to the satisfaction of everyone. The Latin words *religio* and *religare* probably take us to its root meanings of "reverence" (*religio*), and "to tie, to bind" (*religare*). The core idea here is a basic and fundamental tie that binds people together to get them growing in the same direction – an agricultural metaphor. Put another way, religion concerns the spiritual root of existence constituting the ground of unity for human life and society.

When thinking about religious awareness from a biblical standpoint we find that human beings somehow transcend the world in which we exist, living as what C.S. Lewis memorably referred to as a sort of spiritual amphibian. Though we are certainly created for this world (Gen. 1-2), living as dependent creatures in temporal reality, we are clearly made for fellowship with the eternal God, and so we find that eternity is in our hearts (Eccl. 3:11). It is for this reason St. Augustine famously prayed to God, "You have made us for yourself and our hearts are restless until they find their rest in thee."[78] So, from a Christian perspective, human beings, who alone of all creatures can rationally reflect on their condition, are essentially and inescapably religious beings because of the relationship we each sustain to God our Creator and the ineradicable sense we carry of our dependency and accountability.

Religion is therefore much more than the practice of this or that set of rituals. Religion is an all-encompassing reality that may or may not be connected to cultic rites and liturgy – in fact most religious perspectives are not. The philosopher Herman Dooyeweerd argues that the faith function of people's lives, which is subject to God's revelation as the norm for faith,

> ...issues from the religious root of our temporal life, namely the heart, soul, or spirit of a person. Because of the fall into sin, the hearts of human beings turned away from God and the religious ground-motive of apostasy took hold of their faith and of their whole temporal life. Only the Spirit of God causes the rebirth of our hearts in Christ and radically reverses the direction of our temporal function of faith.[79]

Yet no matter how far it has fallen from the truth, "faith is always oriented to divine revelation,"[80] the only question is how people will respond. Thus, from the biblical standpoint, all of life is religion as we either worship and serve the living God in all aspects of life, or, because of our fallen condition, are turned toward the worship of aspects of creation (Romans 1); the honor of surrogate gods, which Scripture calls idolatry.

This idolatry may well take on an ideological character where one or more aspects of creation are identified, and then absolutized as being the root of all meaning and foundation of all explanations. For example, in ideologies like communism the community is absolutized; in rationalism the logical aspect or mind; in individualism the individual; in romanticism the emotional aspect; in economism the economical aspect of creation; in materialism the physical aspect; in evolutionism, the biotic, and so forth. The many isms in Western cultural thought are the surrogate gods of the modern world.

In its broadest sense then, religion is man's answer to God's Word-revelation; it is our varied human response as creatures to our Creator. Every mother's son does give an answer whether we realize it or not. Again, it is not a matter of whether, but which; is our response to God's Word and works one of faithfulness, or rebellion? This answer does not simply determine whether we go to church, mosque, synagogue or temple, it affects how we view marriage and family, human society, education, law and yes, politics and government! It is productive of the differences in how we view all the critical questions of life and social order.

Revelation throws the fire of the antithesis upon the earth. It divides parents and children; it sets friend against friend; it drives rifts within the nation; it turns humankind against itself. "Do not think that I came to bring peace on earth," says the Savior, "I have not come to bring peace, but a sword" (Matt. 10:34).

The Rise of Secularism

Although the provenance of the term religion implies tying and binding together, unity is not typically the first thing people tend to think of when religion is discussed in our time. In fact, the 'ties that bind' have in many ways been cut in modern culture. In the Western world, after the Reformation, and following the religious wars of the sixteenth and seventeenth centuries, a sense of religious unity in the kingdoms and empires of Christendom was increasingly ruptured at the societal level. During the Enlightenment, the notion of a supposedly religiously neutral secular state, built in terms of a rationalistic scientific method, was born, gradually invoking a public-private, secular-sacred separation of life in the name of achieving unity and tolerance for civil society and government.

That this sentiment is still with us and dominates the public discourse is evident from the Dalai Lama's recent book, *An Appeal to the World*, in which this widely celebrated 'global spiritual leader' writes in the opening paragraph, "For thousands of years, violence has been committed and justified in the name of religion...; for that reason I say that in the twenty-first century, we need a new form of ethics beyond religion. I am speaking of secular ethics."[81] He goes on to say that the basis of this new ethic is our fundamental human spirituality! The ambiguity and self-contradiction involved in this claim is obvious – how can a secular ethic grounded in human spirituality be beyond religion i.e. escape fundamental religious assumptions about the world?

We will examine the religious character of this secular spirituality in due course. For now it is sufficient to note that based on what we have observed about the true character of religion, it is impossible for anyone who exercises office in political and civic life to be free from religious conviction – both in terms of their posture toward God and in regard to what they believe is true or false concerning the aspects and structures of reality.

For example, in political life we are immediately confronted with the fundamental questions: what is the meaning of government; what is the source of governmental authority; what is the state; what is the purpose of the state; and what should be promoted and enforced as good and right in society by a just state? For the Lama, the answer to the last question is that the just state would promote 'secular ethics.' But all such ideas about justice and society are shaped by acknowledged or unacknowledged religious presuppositions – in other words by a worldview. To simply speak in general terms of the 'authority' or 'legal competence' of civil government immediately invokes normative states of affairs i.e., the nature of authority, legality and the ground of competency, which all require a religious worldview foundation.

In addition, the religiously motivated move of artificially creating a strict sacred-secular, private-public divide (a dichotomy not found in real people's lives, but imposed upon them) meant that secularism essentially replaced Christianity as the new public faith of the West, the new religion of state, and the ostensible glue holding Western society together. At the same time, by affirming a religious relativism wherein all faiths are to be regarded and treated equally, while in the same breath declaring itself non-religious, secularism brilliantly enthroned itself as the ultimate religious principle.

Our culture thus invokes an abstract dualism that is said to separate 'faith' from the public affairs of civil government in the interest of unity, but which is in fact designed to deprivilege Christianity and thereby protect the religious assumptions of secularism from being challenged. Those assumptions are grounded in a dogmatic belief in the absolute autonomy and independence of human thinking. South African philosopher Danie Strauss highlights the religious motif of these political ideas at the beginning of the Enlightenment:

> The deepest motivation of the new era is found in its conviction that the human being can only proclaim its sovereignty (autonomous freedom) by exploring the possibilities of the new natural scientific understanding of reality…an instrument by means of which it could control and subdue all of reality. This instrument was supposed to serve the purpose of a complete methodological breakdown of everything within reality, introducing the creative capacities of rational thought to once again create order from this resulting heap of chaos…now human reason actually took over the task of creation originally assigned to God by Christianity.…Thus modern humanism ultimately deified the human being, embedded in the new motive of logical creation.[82]

Thus, flowing out of the dominant thought-forms of the Renaissance and then the Enlightenment, the Christian teaching regarding God as the giver of law, the source of truth and meaning for all of life in every aspect, has been replaced by the idea of an ever-expanding autonomy for human affairs – circumstances in which man himself becomes the new creator of order amidst the chaos. As a consequence, the 'secular' character of the West has been taken for granted for over sixty years.

It is nonetheless true, as we have already observed, that 'spirituality' is ubiquitous in our present society, with various pagan beliefs, occultism and Eastern religions flourishing. This does not contradict what we have said so far about the rise of secularism because they flourish, as far as Western people are concerned, within the rubric of the assumptions of a religious secularism. Which is to say, they thrive within a secular interpretation of the nature of reality (autonomy and religious relativism) which has opened up the space for them to be promoted, celebrated and widely practiced.

It is important to remember in this regard, that most non-Christian religion is essentially a form of atheism because these worldviews and ideologies do not posit an infinite, personal and relational God who is distinct from and stationed outside the cosmos, governing history. As such, Eastern religions do not present a challenge to the secular claim of radical human autonomy – indeed they simply reinforce it. The Dalai Lama, calling for a secular ethic beyond religion is the perfect illustration. He claims, "The key to reaching harmony, peace and justice is the sharpening of our awareness of our inner reality by, more listening, more contemplation, more meditation."[83] There is no menace to secularism here, only the comfortable reassurance that all the answers lie within man himself and his autonomous thinking.

The Nature of Religious Secularism

Secularism as religious ideology is a complicated thing to try to define simply. It is like a great river with many tributaries feeding it. At first, the very expression 'religious secularism' might sound to some ears like an oxymoron – since secularists usually think of themselves, by definition, as 'non-religious.' However, we have seen that this is impossible. The influential atheistic thinker Friedrich Nietzsche clearly believed secularization was the route to salvation. He wrote, 'We deny God, we deny our responsibility before God, thereby we save first of all the world.'[84] Secularism is thus held out as a salvific principle.

So, let's consider first the meaning of the word secular. It finds its root in the Latin word 'saeculum,' a noun meaning an age, the Greek word being aion, which in English is aeon. The adjective secular in the history of the West is now associated with a series of dualistic contrasts that came about when Greco-Roman philosophical thought interacted with Christianity and in many respects was synthesized with it. The European philosopher Dirk Vollenhoven argued that much of the history of Western thought is dominated by this synthesis. In fact, Vollenhoven divided the history of Western philosophy into three periods: before the synthesis period (pagan era of antiquity till AD 50); the time of synthesis (patristic and medieval scholastic era); and modern philosophy (1450 onward) which tended to reject or denude the Christian element of the synthesis, emphasising pagan elements. This divergence was manifested in the Renaissance, which emphasized the pagan side, and the Reformation which emphasized the Christian side.[85]

Simply stated, much of Greek thought held that the cosmos consisted of two uncreated substances, eternal form and eternal matter. 'God,' an unmoved mover, was pure form, thought-thinking self. This dualistic idea eventually gave way to Plotinus' Neo-Platonism in which everything that exists emanates through gradations from an absolute undifferentiated blank unity, which he called the One. Whether beginning with an eternal duality or unity, these philosophical abstractions were expressed as eternal forms or ideas and contrasted with matter. As a result, an immortal rational soul was contrasted with body, being with becoming, the spiritual with the carnal. In other words, we are given a two-storey view of reality with an upper storey considered higher (pure), and the bottom storey viewed as lower (even evil). It follows logically that the pagan view stressed disembodiment as the highest level of existence, privileged intellectual contemplation over manual work or creative arts, and idealized philosopher kings. Practically, pagan culture in general viewed the material realm as subordinate to the spiritual or ideal.

The synthesis is found in a medieval Christian culture that more or less embraced this impressive Greek system construing nature as form and matter, while arguing that God's grace was required to bring nature to moral perfection and usher the human person into eternal bliss. The incompatibility of Genesis 1 and John 1 – which tell us that in the beginning a personal and relational God called into being the heavens and the earth – with the speculation of an unmoved mover and eternal matter being wrestled with by Christian thinkers but never overcome. So, the basic religious cosmology of the synthesis era consisted of two realms – nature and grace. The church and its spiritual authority operated in the realm of grace, ministering the sacraments, giving spiritual oversight, and consisted of the sacred vocations ruled by God's revealed Word. By contrast, the world outside the ecclesiastical sphere (nature) was secular and was ruled over by secular authority in terms of a stoic philosophical construct of natural law.

Re-enchanted with the Ordinary

This dualistic view generated a variety of further contrasts. Culturally, a dichotomy was set up between the temporal affairs of the world and the spiritual affairs of the City of God. This led by extension to hierarchical distinctions between occupations and vocations belonging to the upper storey of existence (the spiritual and sacred), like clergy and monks, and those belonging to the secular world of culture and politics. Even great Christian thinkers like Augustine and later Luther tended to reinforce this kind of approach. Of course, it is legitimate to distinguish between the spheres of church and state and their jurisdiction; a non-ecclesiastical sphere of life differentiated by the emergence of an independent church was part of the contribution of Christianity in undermining the priestly claims of the totalitarian politics of the pagan world. But the sacred-secular divide discussed here means far more than identifying and differentiating societal entities.

Rather, I am describing a deformed Christian worldview, deeply informed by Greek philosophy, that has played a significant role in giving us the idea of the secular as an entire domain of creation that falls outside the direct jurisdiction of Christ and His revealed Word. The upshot in the West meant the so-called sacred space of grace was steadily eaten up by the secularizing tendency of the realm of nature – coming to expression in the Renaissance. During the Reformation, however, John Calvin rejected this distinction as artificial and sought to revive the Hebraic roots of biblical faith that saw all of life as an integral religious whole under the living God.[86]

The Canadian philosopher Charles Taylor argues that Calvin's branch of the Reformation tended toward the disenchantment of the world by abolishing a limited sacred realm, and so helped create modern secularism by breaking down a duality that persisted throughout the Middle Ages. This analysis has some merit to the extent that many kicked against Calvin's notion that all of life should come directly under the Lordship of Christ and His Word, thus bringing about a counter-reaction that expanded the so-called secular realm.

But I think Taylor's conclusion that Calvin's thought fuelled the disenchantment of the world is wrong. The seeds of a radically secularizing worldview were clearly present in Greek thought, even in its Christianized, Roman Catholic form – including the power and autonomy of reason and the idea of natural law as a sufficient principle for the secular world. We will see that modern secularism is really a revived form of paganism. Calvin's reformed vision effectively resisted both the ecclesiasticizing and secularizing of life, by freeing all of life to serve Christ, thereby re-enchanting the ordinary life of people in all aspects and vocations with an eternal meaning and spiritual significance. The Enlightenment and Romantic periods were both counterreactions to this biblical Calvinism.

The Church of the Secular

Today of course, the idea of the secular no longer involves the specifics of the two-storey medieval construction of nature and grace. Instead, secularism has become an interpretation of life that regards the living God and his Law-Word as non-essential and irrelevant for life and thought in the modern world. The idea that we need grace in light of the problem of sin is routinely thought of as the powerplay of obsolete organized religion that has inhibited man's true nature and robbed him of his freedom. Guilt becomes a psychological disorder we can be free from by transcending such obstructive religious ideas.

The idea that we have moved beyond the need for God's renewing and restorative grace in Christ has involved a process of gradually distancing the living God from the real world. With the declining power and influence of the ecclesiastical sphere in the West, due in large measure to the pagan forces unleashed during the Renaissance and Enlightenment, people increasingly began to believe in human reason as totally independent of God. Thus, the historian Peter Gay characterized the Enlightenment as "the rise of modern paganism."[87] Accordingly, the things we didn't like about the God of Scripture were steadily stripped away, leaving us with variations of Deism, world-soul pantheism, animistic cosmic forces, or blank atheism. It is not a coincidence that these developments coincided with the rise of pagan notions of cosmic evolution given a scientific veneer by men like Charles Darwin.

These thought currents, combined with the accomplishments of modern science and technology, not to mention social phenomena like urbanization and greater social mobility, left many believing that the personal God of Scripture, a relational and covenant-enforcing God, was unnecessary and indeed unwelcome. Taylor is to the point in tracing the drift: "The slide to Deism was not just the result of reason and science but reflected deep-seated moral distaste for the old religion that sees God as an agent in history."[88]

Clearly, the idea of an impersonal deity uninvolved in historical eventuation is much more amenable to a people increasingly thinking of themselves as autonomous. Since God previously belonged only to a sacred upper storey in any case – periodically interfering in temporal public affairs via the church – perhaps He could be pushed further and further out so that even the spiritual sphere of grace could be liberated from a sovereign Lord and the church itself delivered from the personal covenantal God of the Bible into a new concept of the divine. Enter the God of liberal theology, popularized by the seventeenth-century Dutch philosopher Baruch Spinoza. This god is in fact one with the world; 'God' is merely the indwelling Spirit of an impersonal cosmos. The world is just a self-contained, immanent order, to be understood on its own terms. Hence creation was fully separated from the Creator so that man's reason could rule in the natural, societal and ecclesiastical world.

In this fashion the religion of secularity is seen to be rooted in a worldview which embraces an impersonal mother Nature and autonomous man in a world without historical revelation. Subsequently, that world is perceived not only as impersonal, but increasingly chaotic and mysterious. This irrationalistic turn thought to arrive at a kind of 'original religion' of humanity – a perspective many contemporary secularists hold must be recovered. Taylor comments on this secular concept of an original religion that, if we see it everywhere covered with distorted accretions, this must be because of some degeneration in virtue or enlightenment, perhaps aided by sinister forces which profited from darkness and ignorance (often castigated as priest craft). The differences between religions, which consist in varied such accretions are all false. We must return to the simple underlying common truth.[89]

This is the levelling demand within today's secularism which requires all 'faiths' to submit to becoming one, under the benevolent supervision of the secular state. At the same time it indicates a pivot within secularism from a rationalist to an irrationalist posture.

Pagan Secularity

The initial emphasis of secular thought on a rational but impersonal deterministic order, reaching its zenith in the late eighteenth and early nineteenth centuries, thus gave way to an irrationalistic turn positing mystical nature and subjective experience as the key to reality. These rational and irrational polarities, which are both still with us, expose the clearly pagan roots of secularization.

Following the Greeks, the nineteenth-century Romantic movement emphasized nature as a mystical stream of life – a great esoteric unity within and without. The source of life and meaning was to be found not in rational, mathematical thought, but in feeling and experience. With this in view, humanistic thinkers suggested that instead of positioning man versus nature (reason against feeling), perhaps a higher synthesis and unity could be reached: a unity with nature! A model for this has frequently been the Greeks and their political social order. R.J. Rushdoony has observed that the [Greek] city-state was an esoteric, mystical and divine body with a kind of androgynous wholeness, and the religion of the city state was basically a fertility cult.[90] Interestingly, fascination with gods, goddesses, fertility cults and nature as divine were basic to the European Romantic movement.

We can see then that the varied secularising movements of the Renaissance, the Enlightenment and Romanticism shared in common an underlying hostility to biblical Christianity. They opposed the idea that man is a fallen, sinful being in need of redemption by his Maker, shared a fascination with notions of an infinite universe, impersonal nature and a philosophical chain of being and saw man as the new god of creation in the process of becoming utterly free and realising total autonomy.

Together, these thought currents gave rise to what has been called existentialism – the philosophic atmosphere of the modern secular West. This view frees life and society from any sense of restraint or moral authority that would stand above it. As French existentialist Jean-Paul Sartre commented, "Dostoevsky once wrote 'if God did not exist, everything would be permitted;' and that, for existentialism, is the starting point. Everything is indeed permitted if God does not exist." In a similar vein, the postmodern social theorist Michel Foucault admitted frankly, "For modern thought, no morality is possible."[91]

Ironically then, with a personal God removed from the scene and the universe once again regarded as churning helplessly in endless cycles like socks in the tumble-dryer, modern secular man, as Francis Schaeffer once put it, "has become a mystic."[92] Regarding the living God of Scripture to all intents and purposes as dead, creational meaning vanishing with Him, modern people want esoteric experience so that they might generate from within eccentric personal 'meanings.' Experience as experience is key. The hope is that this inward turn will salvage 'meaning' from the abyss to which rationalistic secular thought has consigned it. But truth, as something objectively knowable in human understanding by virtue of creational law, is ruled out. Inwardness and subjective experience are what count. This existential view represents the zeitgeist of our time. As S.U. Zuidema has pointed out, "over against the adage of the Enlightenment Sapere aude (Dare to be wise) Kierkegaard puts that of Romanticism: Be free, become yourself!" and "subjectivity is the truth." Man's very existence now is freedom itself. You do not become what you are – as though you are something definable by virtue of creation – you only become what you are becoming. Human beings are therefore indefinable! One can only choose (elect) oneself by wanting to be oneself (or not). This is nothing less than a secularized doctrine of the new birth and election which lands secular man entirely in the pagan world of irrationalism. Again Zuidema explains:

> The idea of self-election places man outside the scope of God's law and beyond all lawfulness; it gives the idea of human subjectivity the sovereignty which was stolen from God. The former idea is itself a product of secularization and, as such, has a neo-paganistic character.[93]

The Western secular existential perspective thus leads to the conclusion of the Eastern philosopher. To answer the questions of life, the truest guide is simply inward experience – every insight comes out of new experience. Francis Schaeffer tellingly commented on these looming developments in the West several decades ago:

> What about the spread of Eastern religions and techniques within the West – things like TM, Yoga, the cults? We have moved beyond the counterculture of the sixties...; these elements from the East...are fashionable for the middle classes as well. They are everywhere.... What about the growth of occultism, witchcraft, astrology...? people are looking for

answers – answers they can experience…. Wherever we look
this is what confronts us: irrational experience.[94]

A Secular Utopia

In one sense then, we have made a great intellectual loop in
the Western world. Pagan thinking has boomeranged. We began
pre-Christian and thoroughly pagan. The gospel was effectively
spread by the Patristic church, but Christian theology began to
make room (via a synthesis) for Greek philosophical ideas as
pagans were converted, eventually adopting a dualistic view of
the world with upper and lower storeys within nature (two
substances). This led to the emergence of a 'secular' realm and
a series of artificial contrasts within creation. Subsequently,
with various humanistic movements in the history of Western
thought determined to recover essentially pagan Greek ideals,
the Christian faith was pushed further and further back into a
supposedly private, sacred, spiritual upper storey of reality,
increasingly irrelevant to the real, historical world. In our
time, this 'spiritual' realm is increasingly restricted to the
private thoughts between your ears, not to be uttered in any
cultural arena.

The result for society has been that the rapidly expanding
secular domain has more or less eaten up what was left of the
philosophical construction of a sacred domain – which for
centuries managed (through the public strength of the
institutional church) to influence the values of society as a whole.
In so doing, secularism's impersonal worldview has opened up
the public space to a recovery of numerous forms of pagan
spirituality and practices that do not challenge man's radical
claim to autonomy – all in the name of equality, justice, tolerance
and religious relativism. As BJ van der Walt has written:

> Irrationalism taught that all religions are equally true. Pluralism
> no longer implies just mild but radical relativism…irrationalistic

pantheism and mysticism of the late twentieth century [claims] all paths lead to god. Therefore it does not matter which road the individual selects for his spiritual journey.[95]

So, just like the ancient world, all the cults and gods are welcome, so long as they pay homage to the autonomous freedom of man. All religions (in their inner essence) are equally true, because they are different rivers running to the same sea; different roads to the same mountain peak, different paths leading back to an original spiritual religion of humanity. All human faith traditions are merely man-made, emerging from the chaos of historical development. They are culturally conditioned and therefore transient, temporary phenomena that are historically determined – they are thus relativized.

In our time, this reigning pagan-secular spirit even governs how we think about government. A secular, autonomous vision of man, liberated from the distasteful intrusions of a personal, sovereign God, has meant the obvious necessity of building a utopia – a secular polis – the kingdom of man. The presuppositions of a secular worldview require a political religion capable of absorbing mankind and all his 'faiths' into an immanent One – the pagan state – with its secular ethics and religion of humanity arising from within. Here unity is the supreme secular virtue, and religious division is anathema. This is why the faithful preaching of the gospel of the kingdom God is the one thing that cannot be tolerated, because it destroys man's claim to self-creation, self-election, self-definition and do-it-yourself redemption. The result of thinking about human government, as Schaeffer pointed out, is

...gravitation toward some form of authoritarian government... and the freedoms, the sorts of freedoms we have enjoyed in the West are lost...; the growing loss of freedoms in the West are the result of a worldview which has no place for "people."[96]

Western secularism is ultimately a paradox. As van Houten has argued, "modern society is increasingly displaying the characteristics of the oldest religion that has existed, namely paganism. It seeks to hide its religious character as a means of controlling the 'public' realm, creating a political religion with a totalitarian impulse."[97] Accordingly, what we as Christians face today, in what is sometimes called the 'culture wars,' is a life-and-death struggle between the Christian view of reality and the public faith of religious (pagan) secularism. This confronts us with the critical question: upon whose shoulders is the government – Christ's or the modern state's? Where does authority and sovereignty ultimately lie?

The Increase of His Government

Before we come to a discussion of authority, it is important to highlight how the Christian must respond to the rapid advance of pagan secularism. In terms of how we speak about our culture, we need not say we are a post-Christian people. It is in vogue to do so, but the reality is, we cannot fully undo the profound transformation that the influence of the gospel exerted upon the West over the past two millennia. Biblical faith is deeply embedded in our language, literature, music, architecture, structures of government and social life, laws and art, and cannot simply be flushed away by contemporary intellectuals – culture is more complex than that. Most modern political theory itself in the West has been an attempt to secularize Christian theological themes, so even as Christianity is rejected, our modern pagan secularity is invariably parasitic upon it.

This means our secular paganism is qualitatively different from pre-Christian paganism and carries greater culpability. What we can say is that we are increasingly non-Christian or de-Christianizing. And we should be in no doubt about how serious a matter that is. Today's pagan secularism is probably the greatest crisis that Western Christianity has yet encountered.

Secularism's invasion of the church in the late nineteenth and early twentieth centuries in the form of rationalistic modernism decimated the mainline churches by requiring God's revelation to submit to man's reason. Those denominations who surrendered to modernist secularity are now on life support, closing dying churches weekly. In its irrationalist (existential and postmodern) outfit, pagan secularity is now found deep inside the walls of contemporary evangelicalism where the authority of Scripture, the doctrine of God and creation, and a scriptural view of human identity and sexuality are under serious assault. And, in the face of what appears to be the colossus of a growing neo-pagan vision of a secular statist religion, we are confronted with the grave temptation to various forms of escapism and to a despairing pessimism about the Christian gospel and our life in the world. Naturally many Christians are asking themselves, what are we to do?

The first critical thing Christians must do is resolutely reject the relativism of pagan secularism with its denial of the truth in Christ and his Law-Word for all creation. Secular relativism is self-refuting because it obviously has absolute intent – to control the whole playing field and assert its own absolute truth. We must expose secularism's self-deception and present our culture with biblical truth and a coherent scriptural worldview with clarity, grace and conviction. The scriptures affirm four critical and foundational realities that confront all people:

1. The Triune God

2. His creation

3. His redemptive purposes

4. His Law-Word, which gives direction to the totality of created reality and cannot be finally overturned by man's self-creating illusions.

In this biblical view, creation is meaningful because it is totally dependent, at all times and in every part, on the powerful Word of God which governs all things and relates each aspect of reality to every other aspect in terms of His design and purpose. As such, no 'resting point,' or final explanation for reality can be found within creation itself. In part and as a whole a dependent cosmos points us back to God as the Creator. Consequently, life is meaning-full, because creation is meaningful.

Second, Christians must resist the inward turn that would privatize our faith. It is not sufficient to simply affirm a personal faith in Christ existing between one's ears. We must take an open, public and uncompromising stand with Christ and the truth of the gospel which compels us to openly worship (in thought, word and deed) the living God and reject all false worldviews with our heart, mind, soul and strength. This requires refusing a pietistic reaction to the direction of culture which resigns itself to the status quo. A pietistic response implicitly accepts secularism's false division of reality into public and private, secular and sacred, reason or science and faith and thereby acquiesces to a radically limited role in the world for Christ and the gospel.

To simply affirm biblical truths regarding personal salvation, regularly meet in the church building, and do professional theology is not a sufficient response to the lie seeking to alienate creation from its Maker; this is the lie undermining and threatening our culture. We must confront systematic unbelief with systematic belief, expounding and living out a Christian world-and-life view, grounded in the scriptures, one that unveils the beauty of the treasures of wisdom and knowledge hidden in Christ. And we must do so not simply in private, but in every area of our lives. Biblical faith and life in Christ are not simply a private belief, or an autobiographical comment on subjective experience; they are the truth in Jesus Christ declared to all men and nations which is self-attesting through the power of the Holy Spirit.

Third, we must reject and attack the false dualism of secularity. I have pointed out that Christianity, in the form of a nature/grace dualism, adopted elements of Greek thought, with its own secular-sacred divide; a culture which by the time of the classical Greeks held philosophic secular thought in highest esteem. I argued that from the Renaissance onward, the secular domain began emancipating itself from the sacred domain. Now, the secular not only totally dominates the sacred, but has arrogated to itself a certain sacred character. It demands the radical privatization of all faith except its own. By and large believers fail to see the spiritual significance of this. When people – including Christians – effectively deny that demonic spiritual powers are at work in the idea of a 'secular' worldview, by endorsing and supporting secularization in culture, they become blind to the presence of those powers.

We have seen that secularism is, in a certain sense, the unplanned child of a deformed Christianity that is now betraying its mother and must be corrected to avert disaster. The only way to overcome pagan secularism is to go right to its root and challenge the validity of a religious worldview that thinks God and His Word can be safely pushed out of the real world or corralled into the privacy of the mind alone. We can no longer settle for a synthesized culture, where Christianity is blended with secularism and we are content to live next to pagan secular culture rather than reforming it. In the spirit of the Reformation we must reject this synthesizing mentality.

The Bible recognizes no dualism in creation but only an integral life of love and service to God and neighbor. All of life is religion, not merely one narrow aspect of it. Central to our faith is the unity of God's revelation of the kingdom of God – creation, our fall into sin, our redemption in Christ by the power of the Spirit and the consummation of God's restorative purposes in the renewed creation. There are no isolated 'parts' here, one lesser than the other, no sealed domains impervious to the redemptive power of the gospel. There is no 'secular arena' with diplomatic immunity from the rule of Christ and His Word.

A failure to reject false dualisms and recover an integral scriptural world-and-life-view in our time will make the situation we are facing gravely worse than it already is because, as Zuidema points out:

> The more the church becomes ecclesiasticized, the more it will profane life outside of the church and abandon it to profanation. …This is a problem which, unless it leads man to retrace his steps in this emancipation, will irretrievably abandon us to nihilism and the destruction of every last human worth, human honor, human value and human responsibility.[98]

These are the stakes in our era. If we do not challenge this false dualism at its root, especially in the church, then not only will political idols know no limits and all government be abandoned to godlessness, but the church will go down to destruction in the name of saving its hide.

Fourth, we must apply the gospel to culture in concrete ways. The rejection of pagan secularism must become practical. The truth of God's Law-Word must be applied to all areas of life – from the family, to education, law, politics, business, medicine, science and arts, all for the glory of God and the good of our neighbor. Since all of life is religion, there is a Christian and scriptural way to think and live in all the diverse aspects of created reality, in terms of God's law and norms – a liturgy of life grounded in Christ's redemptive life and purpose.

To be effective in our task and calling we need insight into God's Law-Word in Scripture and His norms, laws and ordinances in creation for every given area and discipline. We cannot be involved in business and economics as Christians without insight into God's norms and laws for economics; or agriculture without insight into God's law and norms for farming; or government without insight into God's law and norms for political life. Digging out these treasures takes effort. The pagan secularists have been hard at work in all of these fields, working out the implications of their religious view for them – marriage, sexuality and identity, economics, education, law and arts and sciences. They have indoctrinated three generations with these ideas and the result has been radical cultural change. What have we Christians been doing?

Clearly, if we are to respond effectively to pagan secularism we need to take the time to learn what it means to be faithful servants of God in these varied aspects of life. That is the excitement and thrill of the kingdom of God. We are called to a task and we are to do everything with all our might to the glory of God. We can only offer an attractive and coherent alternative to pagan secularism if we live out and teach a vision of God's sovereign government of all things that conforms to the Word of God.

In addition, to see this government of God manifest in the various spheres of life we must develop numerous Christian organizations and institutions: hospitals, guilds, arts initiatives, unions, charities, schools, courts of arbitration, political parties, businesses, film studios, universities, research programs, news media and journalism platforms, Internet search engines and much more. We should be deeply involved in all the domains of life outside the institutional church in a distinctly Christian way if we are to challenge pagan secularism. The institutional church is one important aspect of God's kingdom, but the Christian life is not restricted to the life of the church.

The pagan secularists carefully select, use and focus on particular cultural gateways to inculcate and disseminate their worldview and message. Faithful Christians need to be equally organized and focused in utilizing and developing the various organs of cultural life in distinctly Christian and biblical ways, to make known all the laws, norms and ordinances of our sovereign Lord and the redemptive life of the gospel, disseminating a Christian world-and-life view that redirects us in all these things toward true worship and service for the flourishing of life under the government of God.

We need not only Christian lawyers, but a Christian approach to law; not just Christian artists, but art rooted in a scriptural world-and-life view; not merely Christian doctors, but a Christian philosophy of medicine; not only teachers who are Christian, but a truly Christian curriculum; not just Christians in politics, but a scriptural political philosophy. In other words, we must apply our faith and organize against pagan secularism.

Finally, we must affirm that the government of Jesus Christ over all of life applies not to some things, but to all things, not only to some people, but to all people. This simply means recognizing the true jurisdiction of Christ and the gospel of the kingdom over the totality of creation. Abraham Kuyper argued powerfully:

> Religion concerns the whole of our human race. This race is the product of God's creation. It is his wonderful workmanship, his absolute possession. Therefore, the whole of mankind must be imbued with the fear of God...for not only did God create all men, not only is he for all men, but his grace also extends itself, not only as a special grace, to the elect, but also as a common grace to all mankind.... All partial religion drives the wedges of dualism into life, but...one supreme calling must impress the stamp of one-ness upon all human life, because one God upholds and preserves it, just as he created it all.[99]

If we want to breach the wall of the secular pagan lie, we must use the battering ram of a scriptural world-and-life-view that shatters all false dualisms and reclaims all of creation for the glory and government of God, freeing life in all its aspects to be all that Christ intends it to be. As Herman Bavinck writes:

> Spiritual life does not exclude family and social life, business and politics, art and science ... rather it is the power that enables us to faithfully fulfill our earthly calling, stamping all of life as service to God. The kingdom of God is, to be sure, like a pearl more precious than the whole world, but it is also like a leaven that leavens the entire dough. Faith isn't only the way of salvation, it also involves overcoming the world.[100]

Chapter 4

AUTHORITY, SOVEREIGNTY AND THE HERESY OF LIBERAL DEMOCRACY

The Question of Authority

In the previous chapter we began by examining the nature of religion and discovered it to be both inescapable and foundational in all of life. We went on to explore the development of secularism as an all-encompassing religious worldview with roots deep in pagan thought. Today Western people speak of living in a secular society, with a secular government, and I pointed out that these claims are not philosophically neutral, but rest upon very specific religious ideas about the world. The choice finally was between the government of God in life, or that of autonomous man and his experience.

In deciding between these two ideas we are unavoidably confronted with the issue of authority – the authority of human understanding, of the state, of Scripture and of Christians as servants of the living God, living out their faith in the culture. We need to explore the significance of the question of authority and consider what it means for the way we interpret reality and how we approach political life. This question cannot be sidestepped. It confronts us all in every aspect of our lives. Whom and what will we believe, how will we live, and by what standard? Where does final authority and ultimate sovereignty reside in human affairs?

There are a variety of ways we come to know and believe, various activities by which we arrive at our convictions and acknowledge authority. One commonly cited human activity giving rise to a certain kind of authority is that of science. There are numerous sciences – the natural sciences, medical sciences, operational sciences, not to mention what are often referred to today as social sciences, examining things like anthropology, economics, human geography, jurisprudence, linguistics, psychology, sociology and political science. Theology is also an important science where we examine Scripture and the creeds and confessions of the church, to deepen our understanding and insight into them. When certain individuals have spent much time studying a given scientific field, reaching a certain degree of competence or accomplishment, they may establish themselves as an 'authority' in their discipline.

However, when a Christian reads the Bible to discern God's instruction for daily life, prays, or sings the Psalms to meditate on God's Word and engage in worship, it is not a scientific enterprise. The act of believing the Word of God is different from scientific analysis of biblical texts, for example. Moreover, when we live by the Word of God given in creation and inscripturated in the Bible, we do not establish its authority, but acknowledge it. This is because the only kind of word that the God of Scripture who created all things can speak is an infallible one (because there is nothing He does not know fully).

When we grasp the reality of the triune God, we do so in a manner analogous to the way we 'see' the truth of mathematical axioms or logical laws – the knowledge arises in an immediate way, rather than being inferred from other beliefs. Similarly, the truth of God's self-revelation is not inferred from other more basic beliefs but rather, appears to us as indubitable and as certain as any other belief we have about reality.

Nonetheless, there is a deep connection between our believing activity and the analytical conclusions we reach in any of these areas we now call the sciences. This connection is critical. Both historically and in terms of the structure of our thought as human beings, all our scientific or theoretical knowledge is preceded by a more original, primary knowledge. This is the everyday knowledge of experience, of practical, immediate, full and ordinary life in created reality which deepens and grows with time – it is the experience of being human in God's world.

In this everyday knowledge we encounter norms like good and evil, right and wrong, truth and falsehood, and come face to face with the laws of God for creation in every aspect of living. One does not need to be a physicist, for example, to discern a law that causes objects to fall to the ground, nor a psychologist or philosopher to recognize the reality of moral norms that give rise to a sense of guilt and shame when transgressed. We 'know' this reality regardless of whether we can formulate the law of gravity symbolically on a whiteboard or parse out various philosophical views of ethics.

The power of this primary knowledge effortlessly produces a kind of basic trust that is necessary for every other kind of knowledge to be established. All other forms of secondary knowledge must presuppose this basic trust – for without it there could be no science. This trust rests on a fundamental kind of faith knowledge, or what we might call religious knowledge that is inescapable to humans as created, religious beings. This knowledge can be suppressed and distorted, but it cannot be finally evaded or uprooted.

Not that certain thinkers haven't tried. The radical German philosopher Arthur Schopenhauer tried to reduce the entire cosmos, from the human person, to plants, animals, rivers and seas, to pure will, so that everything which appears to us in life as obvious concrete reality is in fact no more real than a dream. Yet, at the same time, Schopenhauer was religiously enraptured by music, art, humanity and the beauty of the natural world – he didn't live like it was a dream. His theoretical philosophical attempt to reduce reality to mindless will was abortive because in the end he had to reckon with the real world that his meaningful pessimistic writing, philosophical logic, love of art and nature, all presupposed as both necessary and primary.[101] After all, if human experience is really just ravenous mindless Will, why would anyone want to take the writings of one expression of that mindless Will seriously? Especially since he argued with other 'mindless Wills,' that his mindless Will was right.

In the final analysis all our knowledge is grounded in a created reality which, as a mystery, cannot be comprehended in its totality by human thought. This is because human thinking itself, and the scientist himself, are part of the creation they are trying to understand: a cosmos held together and fully dependent upon Christ, the Word of God. By divine revelation, we are given primary knowledge of the true origin of all things and the problem of sin which introduced the sense of confusion, dread, ambiguity and anxiety that persists in human life and culture – well expressed in the writing of men like Schopenhauer or the brilliant art of British figurative painter, Peter Howson.[102] Egbert Schuurman draws the important conclusion that:

> This "knowledge" and this "recognition" imply a knowledge whose content is understood by faith. With our minds we cannot get beyond this faith content, because it is itself the foundation of all our thinking. The knowledge that comes from a basic trust…is knowledge in the sense of ac-knowledge, it is knowledge of the heart. This knowledge which concerns the basic direction of our life is given concrete expression in

our faith knowledge, in our assent and obedience to the divine revelation. This faith knowledge keeps every scientific knowledge in its limited, relative, abstract and provisional place.[103]

In every area of human thought there is the danger that people will start to believe and trust in what a given theoretical activity of science says, and so elevate a secondary, provisional form of knowing to the place of primary knowledge. In other words, a person's faith subtly shifts from God to man, from revelation to scientific theories, from basic trust in God's created reality and Word, to human abstractions. The sciences are valuable tools that have the capacity to deepen our understanding of a given area of life, but they cannot displace created reality or revelation, remake the world, or provide primary knowledge – they are a fallible and secondary instrument. Final authority resides only with the Author of all creation, who places human beings in His creation, made in His image, and subject to His Law-Word for all things. This is no less true in biology and history than in political science or theology.

The Concept of Heresy

This distinctly Christian foundational understanding of the relationship of the sciences (various fields of knowledge and inquiry) to belief and revelation is vitally important when considering the problem of heresy, because the heretic is one who seeks to establish independent authority rather than acknowledge it. Here, a secondary form of knowledge acquisition based in personal theorizing and revising of received and accepted Christian doctrine replaces the primary knowledge of revelation to be confessed and believed. The word heresy comes from a Greek word (*hairesis*), the essential meaning of which is a taking or choosing for oneself. So the heretic is one who, in their belief, confession or teaching, has placed their personal, eccentric choice or opinion above that of accepted and received authority – ultimately the authority of God and His Word.

That is why a person engaged even in the science of theology (a discipline with as many metaphysical pitfalls as anthropology) must take great care not to confuse their novel opinion – even if it is a thoughtful and popular opinion – with ultimate authority or primary knowledge. Which is to say, theological concepts and systems are not identical with Scripture. They must be weighed against Scripture and the testimony of the church down the centuries from the time of the apostles. When theologians have conflated their novel ideas with the Word of God itself – with biblical authority – the propagation of heresy is the end result.

The faith knowledge of the heart variously given with creation, manifest in Christ, inscripturated in the Bible, confirmed by the Holy Spirit and acknowledged and concretized by the confessing orthodox church down the centuries is primary knowledge, while theological systems and conceptual models, though vital and helpful in deepening our understanding, are secondary forms of scientific knowledge, provisional, and always in reform.

It is important to note in passing that the early church leaders did not 'choose,' in terms of eccentric opinion, what would be included in the canon of Scripture. Rather they simply acknowledged and formally recognized those texts which had already been received by the churches as carrying apostolic authority.[104] Heresy then, is essentially false teaching which clearly contravenes the biblical Word and orthodox deposit of faith, denying their binding authority. The early church found itself almost immediately battling heretical ideas, arising from creative theologies that sought to fuse Christianity with various forms of paganism. Several of the most important creeds of the church were the product of that battle for a faithful reception of legitimate authority, rooted in Christ and His Word.[105]

Obviously, without a received authority as the basis of orthodoxy, there can be no heresy – the concept would be meaningless! This means that in a culture which rejects, scorns, or makes light of the authority of Scripture, the orthodox creeds and confessions of the historic church, as well as church discipline, the Christian concept of heresy will not be tolerated. In fact, such heresy will be viewed as unimportant, irrelevant or, in the view of some apostate churches, impossible to define.

At the same time however, a new source of authority will subtly replace Scripture (and biblical confessions) within that culture – for authority never disappears but is simply transferred. This new authority will be taken very seriously, and a novel orthodoxy enforced with the tools of discipline adhering to that new sphere of authority – typically the state. So the basic idea of heresy is not dispensed with, rather the form of heresy is redefined.

From the Christian standpoint, all true authority begins with and resides in the sovereign God and His infallible Word. The Lord Jesus Christ declared, 'All authority has been given to me in heaven and on earth' (Matt. 28:18). The apostle Paul makes the same point crystal clear:

> He demonstrated His power in the Messiah by raising Him from the dead and seating Him at His right hand in the heavens – far above every rule and authority, power and dominion, and every title given, not only in this age but also the one to come (Eph. 1:20-21).

To be seated at the 'right hand' is a symbol of absolute and total authority. Thus the sovereignty and authority of the triune God, as creator of all things, in this age and the one to come, is a foundational article of faith for orthodox Christianity. It is therefore no surprise to find that the Apostles' Creed declares:

I believe in God, the Father almighty,
creator of heaven and earth.

I believe in Jesus Christ, God's only Son, our Lord...

He will come to judge the living and the dead

In a similar fashion the Nicene Creed begins:

We believe in one God,
the Father, the Almighty,
Maker of all that is, seen and unseen.
We believe in one Lord, Jesus Christ,
the only Son of God...through Him all things were made...

Notice that these two foundational ecumenical creeds, which summarize the basic teaching of Scripture, affirm that the triune God is almighty and the Creator of all things; that Jesus Christ is Lord and God and the judge of all. In short, they affirm the absolute sovereignty and Lordship of Jesus Christ. To deny Christ this Lordship and sovereignty is therefore heretical.

The Influence of Heresy

Typically, when Christians consider the subject of heresy, we think of church councils, ecclesiastical tribunals and church order – we regard the import of these matters of doctrine as essentially confined to the church institute. After all, what relevance could a person's rejection of Christ's absolute sovereign authority or atoning death for sin have in the workplace or political life, for example? Without doubt, these church-oriented considerations are vitally important for understanding and addressing heresy. The church must confront heretical teaching, refute it, and discipline members.

But what we frequently fail to recognize are the implications of heretical ideas and teaching as they impinge upon life outside the institutional church. This oversight is serious because if we ecclesiasticize the concept of heresy and regard false belief and teaching as having relevance only for the life of the church, we will fail to see how heretical thought profoundly affects other vitally important spheres of life – including the political. In fact, what we believe about Christ's authority and sovereignty actually has far-reaching implications for political life and thought.

In reality, there are times when heretical thinking is only clearly brought to light outside the ecclesiastical sphere where religion is externalized in the rest of life. Because of the tendency among Christians today to acquiesce to secularism's radical dualistic assumptions, one foundational truth about reality is thought to bear authority in the private sphere of the church institute, while a contrary commitment can hold, at the same time, for the public sphere of cultural and political life. Because of this latent dualism, it is possible for fundamental contradictions to persist without the Christian ever clearly recognizing a basic incoherence.

This means that sincere Christians within a confessing church community may believe themselves to be essentially orthodox as far as the essential tenets of the faith are concerned, while at the same time holding to a radical progressive, liberal-democratic or even Marxist view of cultural and political life for the public space – frequently without ever recognizing a basic contradiction with their confession. In short, their ecclesiasticized confession of faith has not been mediated or contextualized to cultural and political life through a scriptural worldview in a systematic, coherent way.

Consequently, on social issues, such believers will frequently suggest to fellow Christians that the state is merely a neutral apparatus to uphold a vague common good, or that things like abortion, the redefinition of marriage or euthanasia are matters of indifference. Worse, they may even suggest that these developments are a good thing for 'society out there.' In these instances, arising either from ignorance or an arrogant setting aside of Scripture, heretical views of God which deny His total sovereignty in all of life have manifested themselves in areas outside the church institute. In the modern church, these cultural matters are left largely unaddressed and so false and incoherent beliefs can remain quietly hidden.

This pervasive influence of heresy is inevitable. Because religious presuppositions are the point of departure for every area of life and thought, not just in the church or the science of theology, heresy never confines its impact or effect within the ecclesiastical sphere. As a result, well-meaning Christians who are inconsistent in their thinking and lack a comprehensive biblical worldview can unwittingly adopt views and practices in other areas of life that are rooted in heretical assumptions. In short, Christians frequently embrace and 'baptize' heretical political theologies and cultural ideologies as suitable for the life of supposedly secular society, often for want of any clearly Christian alternative, and without ever realizing they are in denial of fundamental confessional truths of Scripture and the creeds.

What is Democracy?

Having considered the meaning and influence of heresy, we are now ready to turn to the concept of democracy and attempt to relate the two. It may initially seem somewhat shocking to identify liberal democracy as an expression of heretical ideas. Do I not believe in the consent of the people to be governed, or their legitimate role in the election of their leaders? I do. Do I wish to replace historic democratic institutions with an absolute monarchy or some dictatorial form of government? I do not. I have no desire to do away with the hard-won cultural and political freedoms bequeathed by our Christian forebears in the form of parliamentary or congressional institutions that involve responsible citizens in the election of their political leaders, whether in constitutional monarchies or other free republics.

This being the case, what is really at issue with the question of liberal democracy – the majority view of Western people today? In what sense is the contemporary view rooted in heretical ideas? Clearly, there are a variety of forms (or structures) of political life, even in the Western tradition. Britain has a monarchy, an established church, a House of Lords and Commons. Canada has an upper and lower house (Senate and Commons), with a viceroy for the monarchy called the Governor General. The United States has a President (executive), Congress and Senate. All have an ostensibly independent judiciary. In all these contexts the state is a public legal institution over a particular territory there, to serve the public interest. This is the meaning of the Latin expression, *res publica*. In this sense, the modern state is republican (or a republic) by definition, irrespective of the particular form it takes (constitutional monarchy or otherwise).

So I do not intend to quibble here over the varied and particular structures of Western political life and which form is best; my aim is to address questions of basic religious direction. What is the basis and source of final authority that gives direction to any society? Where does ultimate sovereignty (which is another word for kingship or rule) lie? This inquiry leads inevitably to a vital question: What is the religious root of the contemporary idea of democracy, and is it consistent with the Word of God and orthodox confessions of the church? As Armenian-American social critic Rousas Rushdoony noted, "Behind all this is the question of authority: is it from God, or from man? If God is the sovereign authority over all things, then His Law-Word alone can govern all things."[106] In other words, we are really reduced to three choices for political life; popular sovereignty, state sovereignty, or God's sovereignty.[107]

In a book published in 1955, Lord Percy of Newcastle argued that democracy as ideology is a "philosophy which is nothing less than a new religion." The book was called *The Heresy of*

Democracy: A Study in the History of Government, and it called attention to these foundational questions. The word, democracy, itself is derived from the Greek word *demokratia*, which brings together *demos*, meaning 'the people,' and *kratos*, meaning 'authority' – in popular parlance, people power. The basic underlying idea of radical democracy is popular sovereignty. So the question naturally arises, is popular sovereignty (or indeed state sovereignty) consistent with biblical truth and an orthodox doctrine of God? In a democratic order without God's ultimate sovereignty recognized, is it not the case that man's theoretical political idea of popular sovereignty replaces creational and biblical revelation as the basis for social order? Ideological democratic thinkers like John Dewey held that there was a basic contradiction between the popular sovereignty of man and the absolute sovereignty of God. Christianity and the family were for Dewey essentially aristocratic and anti-democratic and therefore incompatible with his vision of democracy.

To properly answer the question whether modern liberal democracy is rooted in heresy, expressed in the political sphere, it is necessary to briefly do two things. First, we need to consider the religious assumptions of the liberal democratic tradition and where it stands now. Second, we need to consider the specific claims of Christ. From the scriptural standpoint, no orthodox view of political life can negate the claims of Jesus Christ.

The Origins of Liberal Democracy

It will be important for us to deal with the qualifier 'liberal' in the expression 'liberal democracy' as we proceed. Democratic institutions are one thing, the contemporary notion of liberal democratic society is quite another. In the first place, it is important to note that it is misleading to describe Western culture as consisting of democratic societies or democratic states. This is reductionistic because society as a whole is not democratic. As Strauss points out:

> [T]he adjective democratic acquired a new life in its use as a noun, for in this case, the state itself was identified with the substantive democracy, and subsequently it was combined with a wide array of adjectives...liberal democracy...and so on. This practice loses sight of the fact that the adjective democratic has a very limited scope...; the adjective democratic has a much more modest domain of application, restricted merely to the election process as stipulated in the constitution of a just state.[108]

Likewise, most other spheres of Western society, like the family or school, are not democratic entities either – no one voted for me to be a father, and parents do not typically put decisions to their children for a vote. Neither are churches, universities or businesses democracies, but they are very much part of society. The authority of legitimate government is actually dependent upon the nature of the office of government; and in historically Protestant lands, the idea of office-bearing and the co-determining of who will occupy those offices of government did not come about by a revolutionary social upheaval to start society over.

Over many centuries in the English-speaking world, under the influence of Christian faith and customs, an expanding degree of participation of the citizenry in their own government developed as governing authority gradually passed from the private sphere of kings, counts and barons, to a public legal sphere in a unified territory. Inherited rights and forms of political life that empowered ordinary people, not just a landed aristocracy, establishment church clerics, or hereditary monarchy emerged, as a deepening consciousness of the sovereignty of God over all people (king and commoner alike) and the value and rights of all families and individuals came to political expression.

Here, democratic principle did not mean the will of the 51% as criterion for truth and justice (a kind of direct rule by mob), but rather increased separation of powers and societal differentiation, with more and more elected representatives in civil government. In Great Britain, the Houses of Parliament (Commons and Lords – the mother of all parliaments) balanced one another, with the Bishops in the Lords acting as the moral compass of the nation under a monarchy which acknowledged and defended the Lordship of Christ and the Christian faith. After the English Revolution led by the Puritans, more and more freedoms developed for ordinary people.

Because of sin, no system of government is perfect, but over many centuries, the fundamental liberties of democratically-elected representative government (which for centuries did not include many groups within society) emerged in what we now call the Anglo-American tradition. Part of that tradition was the English Common Law, rooted in the scriptures, which, though not the product of popular vote, played a critical role in the development of constitutional life. The English philosopher Roger Scruton once remarked that the English law existed not to control the individual but to free him. Thus, free democratic institutions in themselves are not problematic from a Christian standpoint.[109] Clearly, however, the development of the notion of liberal democracy, following the Enlightenment and the French Revolution, is a much thornier matter than simply affirming a particular mode of electing government.

Defining liberalism itself is not a straightforward task. The term has meant different things to different people. Some see liberalism as free markets, individual rights and small government, while others see it as referring to the welfare state and big government. Although John Locke is often thought of as the father of Anglo-American liberalism, the fact is he never used the term and never called himself a liberal because these concepts were not available to him at the time.[110] The term actually referred to the principles of the French Revolution where it was birthed, and for most of the nineteenth century it was seen as French doctrine. As a result, the English were suspicious and distrustful of it. For many, this *liberale* ideology, was just another word for Jacobinism – and it was viewed the same way in the United States. The Encyclopedia Americana of 1831 explained that the new meaning of the word 'liberal' came from France.

Historian Helena Rosenblatt points out that liberalism's first theorists were the Swiss-French political thinkers, Benjamin Constant and Germaine (Madame) de Stael. Interestingly, both of them were actually suspicious of democracy. De Stael wanted 'government by the best' and Constant wanted strict property requirements for voting. They were not interested in minimizing the power of government; Constant regarded private property as a mere 'social convention' under the jurisdiction of society.[111]

But liberalism was an evolving idea and developed new strands. Soon, German thinkers gave fresh impetus to liberalism through the political economists of the later nineteenth century. Men like Wilhelm Roscher, Bruno Hildebrand, Karl Knies and their disciples attacked the idea of free markets and advocated government intervention and state welfare. These ideas were then disseminated in the English-speaking world to great effect. It was not long before notorious liberal thinker John Stuart Mill was advocating societal reform through socialism and young American intellectuals studying at German universities were joining the attack on free markets.

As the new liberalism was gradually mutating from the older revolutionary version, debates arose on what true liberalism was, and two streams of liberalism developed – one was interventionist or statist and the other was not – tributaries that continue to this day. Many liberals, not just Mill, warmly embraced socialism. Prominent liberal thinker, Leonard Trelawny Hobhouse, argued that socialism "serves to complete, rather than destroy, the leading liberal ideals."[112] The more recent descendent in the liberal genealogy is the Anglo-American development where the word liberal came into common use in the second decade of the twentieth century in the United States. Rosenblatt is compelling in explaining that this was due to Republican progressives in 1912 and Wilsonian Democrats in 1916. To them, the word meant the new, interventionist type of liberalism. Woodrow Wilson called himself 'progressive' in 1916 and 'liberal' in 1917. Although Roosevelt's New Deal would eventually come to represent liberalism of this variety, debates continued over which constituted true liberalism, the interventionist or laissez-faire variety, well into the 20th century. As yet there was little, if any, talk of an Anglo-American liberal tradition with roots deep in English history. This idea was conceived as a result of the two World Wars, the rise of the Anglo-American alliance and the Cold War. The fear of Fascism, Nazism and Communism caused liberalism to be reconceptualized again, this time as the 'other' of totalitarianism. It became necessary to emphasize liberalism's support for individual rights. Because of their 'statism,' France and Germany were now found to have non-existent or flawed liberal traditions. John Locke was inducted as a founding father of the Anglo-American tradition and his espousal of property rights made the core of his philosophy...; the US and Britain joined the liberal tradition late and did so by accentuating certain aspects of it and downplaying others.[113]

This latter version of liberalism is the one that is often recommended or defended today, even by Christians, as the venerable and worthy liberal tradition grounded in 'reason.' It is true that the rationalistic Enlightenment movement idealized reason – which eventually expressed itself radically and politically in the French Revolution and its aftermath, with

English, Dutch, German, French and Genevan thinkers all contributing directly or indirectly to an abstract and contractarian political vision – including John Locke. The radical *liberale* of the Revolution was subsequently tamed to a degree in these later versions, mutated and broken into various streams. But is this latter revised Anglo-American version of liberalism really any closer to a Christian view of society, and isn't the older, elitist, socialist iteration once again in ascendancy?

The Rise of the New Old Liberalism

In an illuminating article, the Jewish philosopher and political theorist Yoram Hazony defined this liberalism broadly as referring "to an Enlightenment political tradition descended from the principal political texts of rationalist political philosophers such as Hobbes, Locke, Spinoza, Rousseau, and Kant, and reprised in countless recent works of academic political theory elaborating these views."[114] Crucially, he goes on to identify three core religious axioms that undergird the new liberal-democratic thinking: 1. The availability and sufficiency of reason; 2. The (perfectly) free and (perfectly) equal individual; 3. Obligation arises from choice.

The critical concern that emerges from this analysis for Hazony is that "there is nothing in this liberal system that requires you, or even encourages you, to also adopt a commitment to God, the Bible, family or nation."[115] In fact, none of the foundational forms of primary knowledge discussed earlier actually give shape to the principles of liberal democracy of any stripe. Despite the oft-heard claim that liberal democracy is there to protect traditional belief and historic Christian institutions in a separate sphere of 'privacy,' so as to ensure no one is coerced to be a Christian or live their life in the confines of the Christian view of the traditional family, "everywhere it has gone, the liberal system has brought about the dissolution of these fundamental traditional institutions."[116]

Why is that? Hazony says the answer is not difficult to find. In essence, although liberalism claims to be a form of government that ensures a wide range of individual freedoms:

> ...liberalism is not a form of government at all. It is a system of beliefs taken to be axiomatic, from which a form of government can, supposedly, be deduced. In other words, it is a system of dogmas...about the nature of human beings, reason, and the sources of moral obligations that bind us...; there are no grounds for the claim that liberalism is merely a system of 'neutral' rules, a 'procedural system' that can make traditional political and religious structures work all the better while leaving them intact. Liberalism is a substantive belief system that provides an alternative foundation...[that] has not co-existed with earlier political tradition, rooted in the Bible, as we were told it would. It has rather cut this earlier tradition to ribbons.[117]

Samuel Burgess likewise notes, "Both liberalism and socialism have sought to exorcise religious belief from politics in their own way,"[118] only to replace it with their own religious confessions. The construction of an alternate belief system to Christianity to forge a new type of society is to be expected from the children of the Enlightenment and the French Revolution. As Guillaume Groen van Prinsterer pointed out, "The Revolution, with its variety of schools of thought and its successive historical manifestations, is the consequence, the application, the unfolding of unbelief. The theory and practice of unbelief shaped the philosophy and the Revolution of the eighteenth century."[119]

But a very serious problem arises when the people of God, especially those who are in teaching and leadership roles in the church, downplay, ignore, or even support the dogmatic religious assumptions that undergird the liberal democratic ideal. Despite its evident anti-Christianity on display in our time, marginalizing and persecuting the faith out of the public space, Christian leaders and thinkers are frequently at pains to defend liberal democracy as a 'neutral' and purely 'procedural' system. As we will see, such a claim to neutrality is badly misguided and continues to do great damage in our culture. Edmund Burke, one of Britain's greatest parliamentarians, a contemporary of William Wilberforce and author of *Reflections on the Revolution in France*, believed that the Christian faith was the only true basis for civil society and the source of all good and comfort. He openly challenged the emerging liberal idea of neutrality in political life. For Burke the sovereignty of God was the source of all delegated human power and authority.[120] He saw this biblical view of society under assault by the French *philosophes* and revolutionaries – a revolution which proved to be the mother of many subsequent political revolutions in Europe and beyond. Burgess comments that "In Burke's eyes it was not just the law of man, but the law of God that the revolutionaries were violating. If *Reflections* is concerned with a contract between the living, the dead and future generations, it is equally concerned with the contract between Heaven and Earth."[121]

The French *philosophes* denied that society is an historical-cultural development, God-given and subject to His norms and providential sovereign government. Rather, they saw it as the result of a rational social contract made by free and autonomous individuals. Burke recognized that, beneath the veneer of their liberal discourse concerning equality, liberty and brotherhood, the Revolutionaries were pursuing the elimination of the Christian faith from every sphere of life. The *philosophes* were radical de-Christianizers and the Revolution put their vision into action. For them political order was not something to be normed by creational law, inherited or received, but established by their idea of reason.

Burke understood that the hostility engendered by their cult of reason would not end with an assault on the Christian church, but rather – given the attempted destruction of the Christian faith as a whole – would also come with an assault on property, genuine liberty, and life. The sheer brutality of the Revolutionary period in the destruction of churches, civil freedoms, political opponents, property and lives in a vindictive bloodbath that ended in the Napoleonic dictatorship, bears out these concerns.

As we have seen, the French *philosophes* were picking up and extending the intellectual legacy of various Enlightenment thinkers, including elements from Locke, a child of the English Civil War – who is often burdened with the dubious honor of being a founding father of liberalism, which, as we have noted, is somewhat anachronistic.

That said, Locke's thought, which influenced both Rousseau and Voltaire, was rooted in the Enlightenment rationalistic ideal of mathematical reasoning – a thought process in which most of the sciences were effectively reduced to the numerical aspect of reality. That is to say, rationalistic political theorists hoped they could demonstrate that political life could likewise be reduced to a kind of mathematical demonstration. Government could surely be developed and grounded in terms of clear, rational principles. This they thought could be done in an essentially neutral fashion that would be independent of any religious commitment or historical-cultural baggage. These thinkers believed their vision was based on 'self-evident' facts, clear to all rational people. In pursuing a basic moral axiom that every 'rational' person could agree on, Locke himself provided the rudimentary building materials for the idea that all people are perfectly free, autonomous, and endowed with natural rights.

Although Locke was evidently not trying to develop a sweepingly secular, liberal democratic society, his thought gave inspiration to more radical thinkers because he had needlessly set aside God's creational and moral order in pursuit of the illusion of religiously neutral 'facts.' Locke was supplanting creational and biblical revelation by making man's reason, rather than the Word of God, the basis of justice and civil concord. Even the older pre-modern idea of natural law as something external and given was now jettisoned in favor of natural rights that emerged from man's reason.[122] Shades of the contemporary liberal democratic perspective can be detected in Locke's words:

> The state of nature has a law of nature to govern it, which obliges everyone: and reason, which is that law, teaches all mankind, who will but consult it, that all being equal and independent, no one ought to harm another in his life, health, liberty, or possessions.[123]

This view of the human person as essentially a rational soul, morally obliged to a law of reason, both independent and equal (in a pseudo-mathematical sense) is nowhere to be found in Scripture. In biblical faith, man is a fallen sinner. His human understanding (or reasoning) is distorted and depraved by rebellion against God, often leading him radically astray and he is anything but independent and autonomous.

The Myth of Neutrality

From the Christian standpoint, man is under law in every area of life and not only is he dependent upon God and subject to Him in the totality of his being but he is set in profound mutual interdependence with other people – including those long dead who shaped the culture and customs of the society in which he lives. According to Scripture, a person's whole life is embedded in a created and covenantal reality that immediately relates us to God and then to others in mutual society from the moment of birth.[124]

People are emphatically not voluntary participants in a religiously neutral, self-evidently rational society, created by the contractual fiat word of abstract individuals in an idealized state of nature. Rather, all people are set in families, cultures and societies, made as image-bearers of God, having equal intrinsic value and worth, equally subject to God's law in all things and equally in need of Christ's redemptive life and work. But biblical faith nowhere says all people are perfectly free, rational and equal in the rationalistic sense, nor are they independent of pre-existing familial and social duties and obligations. As Hazony notes:

> Whereas Hebrew Scripture depicts human reason as weak, capable only of local knowledge, and generally unreliable, liberalism depicts human reason as exceedingly powerful, offering universal knowledge, and accessible to anyone who will but consult it. Similarly, whereas the Bible depicts moral and political obligation as deriving from God and inherited by way of familial, national and religious tradition, liberalism makes no mention of either God or inherited tradition, much less specific traditional institutions such as the family or nation.[125]

Locke's faulty assumptions about the human person inescapably led to faulty assumptions about political life. Government itself can now become a creation of the people, beholden to the people and dissolvable by the people, for it is simply a contract between free, independent and equal individuals. Moreover, in keeping with these philosophical axioms, Locke wanted to neatly keep the concerns of church and state totally separate, because like the social contract in public political society, the church is just another kind of voluntary society occupying the private space. The affairs of religion and the affairs of the magistrate are supposedly entirely unrelated. The state (the public area), is ostensibly free of metaphysical religious claims and so in theory should leave the 'private' sphere of religion to organize and go its own way. Burgess' analysis of this naïve position is telling:

> Locke consistently attempts to avoid the conclusion that in disputed cases the state may need to take its own theological character seriously.... [T]he state is not a neutral arbitrator, but necessarily has its own ethical and indeed theological values so the citizen is at times confronted with a clash of civic and religious duties.... And herein lies one of the fundamental problems faced by modern liberal democracies: they have forgotten that their own beliefs are theological in nature and not simply the product of reason. The idea of human beings as bearers of natural rights is not a theologically neutral position. The state makes judgements as to which expressions of religion are acceptable in the public sphere according to its own theological account of humans as rational, autonomous beings who are equal and bearers of natural rights.... [T]he assertion of subjective rights is incoherent without the theological roots of those rights.[126]

Locke thus failed to appreciate that a functional separation of institutions does not preclude religion occupying a central role in civil and political life. Like modern liberals, he simply overlooks the fact that his own beliefs did not emerge from an autonomous, abstract, independent reason. The idea of basic inherent rights (like property rights, conscience rights, right to a fair trial etc.,), along with duties and responsibilities for all people in human society arose gradually in a Christianized culture, where human persons were viewed as God's image-bearers.

The contemporary misplaced belief that the 'truth' of liberal, egalitarian democracy is evident to all reasonable people of goodwill, because it arises from a supposedly religiously neutral public reason (and thus should be the basis of all valid government), ironically leads to a remarkable degree of intolerance. With the French Revolution, these assumptions produced a ferocious anger toward Christian people and churches, despite explicit legal provisions for freedom of religion! As revolutionary liberalism mutated, intolerance to Christianity has proven intractable. This leads us to a consideration of current liberal democratic thought and its claim to sponsor the human rights of all citizens over and above the promotion of any particular conception of the good.

Today's Liberal Democracy

Many modern liberal thinkers took up this Lockean logic, pushing it to much greater levels of abstraction, but perhaps none more notable than the American thinker John Rawls. Rawls looked to refine for the twentieth and twenty-first centuries the rationalistic and contractarian thinking of Locke, Rousseau, and Kant. Like his predecessors, Rawls begins with an idol – an abstract rational man, free and equal, possessing natural rights from which we can supposedly deduce a rational form of government. He offers no metaphysical validation for his claims about the human person; they are creedal, dogmatic statements of belief. For Rawls, man is a political animal, justice is 'fairness,' and reasonable, rational citizens will support his 'just' view of society that is based on the overlapping consensus of reasonable individuals, not theological foundations from revealed religion. Since reason is supposedly public (and neutral), arguments should be framed on those neutral terms, in a manner that everyone might agree on:

> Any comprehensive doctrine, religious or secular, can be introduced into any political argument at any time, but I argue that people who do this should also present what they believe are public reasons for their argument. So their opinion is no longer just that of one particular party, but an opinion that all members of a society might reasonably agree to, not necessarily that they would agree to. What's important is that people give the kinds of reasons that can be understood and appraised apart from their particular comprehensive doctrines.[127]

Rawls either does not appreciate or is unwilling to acknowledge that 'reasons' cannot be properly appraised or understood outside of the comprehensive doctrines (or worldviews) from which those 'reasons' (to be comprehensible) arise, nor does he acknowledge that his own perspective on the just society is itself a comprehensive doctrine.

Christians can certainly offer reasons for their political arguments that non-Christians may well agree with, but not for the reasons Rawls thinks. Unfortunately, his confused view inevitably leads to the incoherent situation inherent in modern liberal democracies today – that there can be no public privileging of any one religion, except secular liberal democracy and its notion of public reason. This doctrine necessarily enforces the interiorization and relativization of non-secular religious belief. Christianity can have a voice only insofar as it can make common cause with Islam, Buddhism, Hinduism or paganism, and that only when it enters the discussion in terms of a public reason the secular liberal can accept.

Like Locke, Rawls seeks to banish religious belief from the sphere of government but does so by arguing for a distinction between privately held religious beliefs and common 'reason.' Beliefs that are allegedly not obvious and evident to the common public reason of other citizens are ruled out of bounds for political life. But as we have seen, this just begs the question: what is reasonable, fair and just, and by what standard? Moreover, who has the right to decide what are private beliefs and what constitutes common reason? In what sense and on what grounds are Rawls' beliefs about humanity as rational, free and equal, or his immanence perspective on justice as 'fairness,' to be regarded as public and the Christian view of man as God's image-bearer subject to transcendent laws of justice merely private? In reality, liberalism is a comprehensive doctrine which simply asserts itself over the Christian faith and tradition, despite being a supposedly naked political conception.

The net result is that the influence of Christianity is deliberately and severely limited by liberal democracy within its political-orthodox confession of man as a reasonable, equal being, in possession of natural rights ascertained by the reason of the sovereign common people. Yet a radically denuded, abstract concept of man as rational, atomistic, asocial, equal, free and solitary is an idol that bears no relationship to created reality and which places man, either individually or collectively, in the position of ultimate sovereignty – the creator of rights, authority and government in terms of his idea. Freedom for Christianity exists here only insofar as its truncated and interiorized confession leaves untouched and unchallenged the basic premises of the liberal contractarian creed. Institutions and organizations which challenge this creed today are under threat because liberal democracy must isolate and destroy the challenge to secular man's sovereignty. If possible, dissenters must be cured of their religious disease in public school. As Jonah Goldberg has pointed out:

> Beneath the individualistic rhetoric lies a mission for democratic social justice, a mission [John] Dewey himself defined as a religion. For other progressives, capturing children in schools was part of the larger effort to break the backbone of the nuclear family, the institution most resistant to political indoctrination.[128]

Within the contemporary liberal democratic views of both popular and state sovereignty, rooted in autonomous human reason, we see secularist theories in political science (remember the sciences are a secondary area of knowledge acquisition) taking the place of creational and biblical revelation, being fashioned into new articles of faith to underpin social order with democratic liberalism becoming an impersonator of primary knowledge and a new confession of faith.

This religious confession has Christianity as its primary target. The Italian political philosopher and politician, Marcello

Pera, has observed, "Since Christianity is the religion proper to Europe and the West, it is Christianity that liberalism wishes to banish to the private sphere or to oppose as an important religion and public point of reference."[129]

Today, this political faith is ubiquitous, permeating every aspect of people's lives. The Polish political philosopher, Ryszard Legutko, writes with insight:

> What we have been observing over the last decades is an emergence of a kind of liberal-democratic general will. Whether the meaning of the term itself is identical with that used by Rousseau is of negligible significance. The fact is that we have been more and more exposed to an overwhelming liberal-democratic omnipresence, which seems independent of the will of individuals, to which they humbly submit, and which they perceive as compatible with their inmost feelings. This will permeates public and private lives, emanates from media..., expresses itself through common wisdom and persistently brazen stereotypes, through educational curricula from kindergartens to universities and through works of art. This liberal-democratic general will does not recognize geographical or political borders.... [T]he liberal-democratic general will reaches the area that Rousseau never dreamed of – language, gestures and thoughts...; this will ruthlessly imposes liberal-democratic patterns on everything and everyone...[130]

This oppressive reality brings with it the overwhelming temptation for believers to attempt a synthesis of liberal democracy with Christianity. Just as the second century Gnostic philosopher and heretic Carpocrates sought a synthesis between Greek thought and the Christ of Scripture, the modern Christian is perpetually at risk of accommodating Christ the Lord to the pretensions of liberal democratic reason. The Carpocratians had statues of Jesus, Pythagoras, Plato, and Aristotle together in their shrines. For them Jesus was a man of pure soul, a wonderful philosopher, and anyone had the potential to rise to His level or surpass Him. But He was not the sovereign creator, redeemer and Lord, the 'ruler of the kings of the earth' (Rev. 1:5). This Greco-Roman Jesus had a shelf-life only as long as that particular synthesis culture lasted. Once that culture collapsed, the relevance of their imaginary Gnostic Jesus disappeared with it.

In the same way, if we reshape Jesus Christ in terms of the liberal democratic general will, reduce Him to the servant of man's political reason or relegate Him to an artificial private sphere with every other religious teacher and philosopher, our relevance, and that of the truncated gospel we preach, will disappear with an apostate society, just like the heretics of the past.

The Claims of Christ

This brings us to our concluding concern – the unequivocal claims of Jesus Christ. The imperial prerogatives of Christ are undeniable and clearly set forth in Scripture, being as plain as the doctrine of God.[131] Consider for example the references to Christ in Scripture as 'the Lord of glory' (Jas. 2:1); this was a term reserved for absolute royal power set forth in the great ancient kings and emperors who thought themselves representations of God in time. When King Herod, dressed in brilliant garments to reflect the sun, which according to Josephus were made of silver, stood in the temple and sought to claim glory for himself, he was struck down by God (Acts 12:21-24).

The ambassadorial command Christians received from the true Lord of glory in the Great Commission of Matthew 28 states and presupposes the absolute authority of Christ to possess and rule the nations (cf. Ps 2). A little later in Acts 2, blazing fire, a biblical symbol of glory, appeared over the heads of the disciples at Pentecost as they were empowered and equipped by the Holy Spirit for the task of spreading this evangel of the kingdom. The idea that this Great Commission and great empowering was intended for a purely interiorized faith or limited private 'religious sphere' as defined by a liberal or pagan state is fatuous:

> The ascendancy of the King of Glory, Jesus Christ, to all pretended kings of glory is most obvious. To suggest that Christ's realm should be controlled or licensed by pretenders is absurd and blasphemous. The modern state, through many symbols, claims to be the bearer of true glory.... The New Testament tells us that Jesus Christ is the Lord of Glory. It is thus the duty of the modern state to let Him in and to submit to Him, not to control Him.[132]

The gates of all life, including political life, must be lifted up to let Him in, or they will be broken down (Ps. 2; 24)! All spheres of human authority are conferred and derived from the triune God,[133] being subject at all times and places to the sovereign and absolute authority of Christ the Lord, in terms of His Word.[134]

This is a far cry from the popular perspective, even in the church of our era. With today's religious confession asserting a liberal-democratic general will – where man's reason and his political society is sovereign and in which morality and justice are created by the state (as reason incarnate), not revealed by God – we are witness to what Herman Dooyeweerd called "a strong revival of the ancient pagan conception which claimed all of life's spheres for the state, considered all morality to be state morality and was therefore not aware of the problem of the relation between individual conscience and state law."[135] There has clearly been a radical departure from our Christian moorings in acknowledgment and confession of the sovereignty of God in Jesus Christ for human society. As Abraham Kuyper observed, "Christian Europe has dethroned the One who was once its King, and the world city has become the queen under whose scepter people willingly bow down."[136]

In substance and content, these secular liberal dogmas are heretical in the assertion of both popular or state sovereignty and their implicit or explicit denial of human sin and fallenness, the salvation and Lordship of Jesus Christ and total sovereignty of God. The cry of eighteenth century liberalism, 'Vox populi, vox Dei' (the voice of the people is the voice of God), echoing down to the present and informing the thinking of our era is heresy, and is no less so because, as political doctrine, it is unlikely to get a Christian into trouble with their local presbytery, diocese or elders. The liberal account of sovereignty, uncritically adopted for the public space by so many Christians today, has a poor record of preserving freedom, justice and human dignity for persons made in God's image – just consider things like the redefinition of marriage, abortion, euthanasia, pornography, confiscatory taxation, poverty and delinquency driven by an assault on the family and new speech codes with their novel 'hate' crimes.

With all its emphasis on human autonomy, liberalism seeks to recreate society in the image of a rebellious and sinful humanity. With Edmund Burke we must be quick to remind fellow believers and our culture at large that neither monarchs, parliaments, senates nor the assembled masses, are ultimate sovereigns. To deny total sovereignty to Jesus Christ in every area of life, like all heresy, is an act of rebellion against God.

Groen van Prinsterer, the Dutch statesman and founder of the Anti-Revolutionary Party in the Netherlands in the years following the French Revolution, issued this warning:

> In its essence, the Revolution is a single great historical fact: the invasion of the human mind by the doctrine of the absolute sovereignty of man, thus making him the source and centre of all truth, by substituting human reason and human will for divine revelation and divine law. The Revolution is the history of the irreligious philosophy of the past century; it is, in its origin and outworking, the doctrine that – given free reign – destroys church and state, society and family, produces disorder without ever establishing liberty or restoring moral order, and, in religion, inevitably leads its conscientious followers into

atheism and despair.... For Christians of whatever church there is now a common cause. They have to maintain Christian faith and law against impiety and anarchy. But if they are to be adequate for this task, nothing less than Christian truth is required.... [T]he Gospel is, and always will be, the ultimate anti-revolutionary principle. It is the sun of justice that after every night of error, appears over the horizon and scatters the darkness. It destroys the revolution in its root by cutting off the source of its deceptive reasoning.... [W]e must take up once more the work of the Reformation and continue in it...; the Reformation put the Christian principle – obedience out of love for God and as the servant of God – into practice, and when in every sphere it placed human authority under God's authority, it validated power by putting it back on its true foundation.... [T]he Revolution starts from the sovereignty of man; the Reformation starts from the sovereignty of God.[137]

In saying these things I do not claim that Scripture gives us a fully worked out political model to be simply read off the pages of the Old and New Testaments where human thought and creativity is not involved, but the Bible does give us a detailed perspective on reality from which, in conjunction with a careful study of creational norms manifest in historical political reality, a distinctly Christian view of political life can be developed. For example, in applying the sovereignty of God, a Christian politics will delimit all power and authority, rejecting the totalitarian impulse whereby civil government swallows up the rest of society in parts-to-whole fashion. By embracing freedom in Christ and the liberty of life this brings, and by recognizing that in the kingdom, God grants talents and gifts He expects to be used, invested and improved for His glory, a Christian political vision will promote free markets, with just weights and measures.

Likewise, by recognizing the reality of sin, a Christian view of government will be skeptical of all radical libertarianism and utopianism. Further, in appreciating our creaturehood and finitude, a Christian politics will seek to conserve what is good and true in cultural life, and from faithfulness to the law of God Christian political thought will commend justice in the courts, care for the poor and oppressed, and charitable welfare for the needy and downtrodden. In addition, from the apprehension of God's law-order in the entire cosmos and all spheres of life emerges a Christian political insistence on the rule of law and an ordered society with peaceful transfers of power.

While it is true that historically no single political party has had a monopoly on religious truth (for Scripture is the standard, not the so-called right or left), some political theories are clearly derived from and grounded in a biblical worldview, while others are not. Some views are built around the scaffolding of the Christian tradition, while others seek to break it down. The good news for Christians labouring in the political sphere is that because a scripturally derived view of political life, informed by biblical prescriptions, bears fidelity to created reality, its fruit will commend itself to unbelievers on its own merits, even where people have theoretically rejected the foundations on which they are built. Mercifully, sinful man is not wholly consistent, which means that, in order to enjoy the fruit of Christian social order, even those who have rejected the faith can and will in many cases recognize the effectiveness and value of its principles.

Now, in an era of liberal democratic heresy, we may take our stand with Carpocrates or with Christ, with the sovereignty of man or with God. Only one of these has a future.

Chapter 5

THE CHURCH, THE STATE AND THE KINGDOM OF GOD

The Practical Reality

Having considered the basic antithesis between the Lordship of Christ and His Word and the rule of autonomous man and his ideas within society, we are immediately confronted with the practical question of the Christian's calling in regard to politics. This is especially acute with respect to the life of the institution of the church and its relationship to the rest of culture. It is not uncommon for confusion and suspicion to quickly arise among Christians when anyone suggests that Christ's Lordship has concrete implications for political life. Does this imply the hammer of a clergy-governed theocracy coming down upon a nation? More broadly and often struggling to frame the questions properly, modern Western Christians frequently wrestle with whether the church should involve itself in political matters or regard itself as an essentially private 'spiritual' realm that does not occupy its time with 'secular' issues? In short, if God's people are to be involved in politics in some way, what is this meant to look like? These are thorny problems that have become increasingly important for Christians to grapple with as Western culture has continued apace to repaganize.

A False Dilemma

For the most part, believers tend to think that they are confronted with a very restricted choice in these matters: either pursue a return to a form of the ecclesiastical culture of Christendom where power and authority over various cultural and political matters is restored to a particular church denomination, or accept that we now live in a post-Christian age where the only thing Christians can realistically hope for is being one of many interest groups in a diverse, multicultural society, with perhaps a seat at the table – a chair pulled out for us by a humanistic secular state now to be embraced as the norm for human society.

Of these limiting alternatives, the second view presently dominates modern evangelicalism. It has therefore become popular in Christian circles to follow the culture in bashing the Roman Emperor Constantine as a bogeyman – the founder of a wholly bad Christendom model in Western history. It is also a way to score easy points in academic circles, since it conforms to the orthodox conventions of critical theory in the universities. As a consequence, any Christian who desires and works to see a strong influence for the Christian faith shaping cultural and political life risks being accused of being "Constantinian" – and is therefore also regarded as a potentially dangerous theocrat, ominously lurking in the wings of history for an opportunity to destroy people's liberties and oppress them. Such a perspective is not only ignorant but a base ingratitude for the incalculable blessings that came to the Western world through the ecclesiastical culture of Christendom, not merely in terms of visible architecture for tourists, but the development of a free university, freedom of the church, canon law and Christian law codes, hospitals, a rich and astonishing legacy of music and art and much more besides. There is certainly a great deal for the believer to be thankful for in looking back on the Christianizing of the ancient emperor in Byzantium – most notably the cessation of a terrible and protracted persecution of Christians.

A tragically common response to pointing out such benefits is the glib romanticizing of political persecution as an ideal state for the church by Western believers who have never experienced it – which is, to put it mildly, naïve. Worse, to pretend to wish for such a situation in the name of spiritual health or growth for the church in our time is the epitome of zeal without knowledge and not knowing what spirit we are of (Prov. 19:2; Luke 9:55-56). The apostles urged the church to pray for political leaders and all those in high positions so that Christians would be left in peace to live quiet, godly lives. They did not intercede for state-sanctioned persecution for the sake of church growth or rooting out nominalism in Christian congregations (1 Tim. 2:1-2). In fact, Paul used his political rights as a Roman citizen to escape flogging and persecution and legally appealed his own case all the way to Caesar to avoid execution by the Jews (Acts 22:25ff; Acts 25:1-27). While they endured courageously, the early church clearly did not view persecution as an ideal state for believers, and the fourth century Christians would have regarded the conversion of the emperor Constantine as a mighty work of God's deliverance – which it most certainly was!

That being said, it must also be readily recognized that the transition from a state of political persecution in the early centuries to what relatively quickly became one of power and wealth for the heads of some of the churches under Constantine and many of his successors brought with it a great many temptations which became the occasion for gradual internal decay within the church – just as the temptation to compromise with progressive culture for the easy life in the West is a cause of internal decay in modern evangelicalism. Moreover, though leaving *internal church affairs* to the bishops, Constantine believed he was appointed by God as the *bishop for external affairs.* And, while he did many good things, like the revolutionary ending of a bloodthirsty death cult in the frenzied arenas of the Roman Empire, the long term results of his conflation of church authority and civil governmental power were very mixed, both in the East and West. He unquestionably set the stage for a historical conflict between church and state. Right up to this day, the Orthodox church is built on governmental authority, and prior to the Russian Revolution, the Czar had the same power in the Russian church as Constantine had claimed for himself.

The result of this early misunderstanding of the church's proper function produces difficulties in discerning the jurisdiction and calling of the Christian church in relation to the rest of society (especially the state) that have revealed themselves again and again. For example, Sean Field, history professor at the University of Vermont, in an article on the rise of royal power in France, noted that by the end of the Capetian period in 1328, "France…was imagined as a 'new holy land' and the French as a 'new chosen people,' with the royal family appointed to defend the kingdom on God's behalf."[138]

France was not the only European power in the Late Middle Ages and beyond with the habit of inappropriately conflating the church institute, the state, and the kingdom of God. Especially in the decades immediately prior to the Reformation, there was a profound lack of clarity among Christians surrounding the character, task and jurisdiction of the church as it relates to God's kingdom on earth – and much confusion persisted even after the Reformation. At this present time, a profound fog of confusion has descended and thickened among Western evangelicals around the same issue, with significant consequences resulting for God's people as society continues to de-Christianize at an alarming rate.

To address this problem, the first task will be to consider the *nature* of the church in its relationship to other social entities and societal institutions – with a particular focus on the state. This will of necessity involve exploring the church's relation to the biblical conception of the kingdom of God. I hope to show that choosing between a revival of the ecclesiastical culture of Christendom and the acceptance of a radically relativized place for Christianity and the church in a normalized secular culture is a *false dilemma*. Which is to say, these are not the only ways of thinking about the church and the role and responsibility of Christians in relation to political life. The journey will involve untangling some theological and philosophical knots and escaping a historical maze of confusion regarding the church and her important relationship to other God-ordained spheres of life.

Confusing the Role of Church and State

As hinted already, the challenge of properly situating the church's relationship to the rest of human society and the broader concept of the kingdom of God is best illustrated by exploring the longstanding struggle between the church and state. In fact, it is the very best place to start because this issue has been critically important in shaping ideas about the nature of the church, the character of national cultures, and the regulation of socio-political life in the West.

At the outset, it must be readily acknowledged that the institutional church has frequently claimed a role for itself in politics that goes well beyond what Scripture teaches about the life and function of the *instituted church* within a social order. Abraham Kuyper observed:

> While we...may not place church and state over against each other as two heterogeneous powers, history shows how very difficult it is to define the correct relationship between the two.

Both of them are to blame for this. It is certainly not only the heroes of the state that restricted the rightful position of the church; there were just as many attempts on the part of the church to *extend its power beyond legitimate boundaries.* The old battle between pope and emperor continued after the reformation, albeit in a different form.[139]

During the history of Christendom, ecclesiastical authorities often sought to accrue to the church institute, powers and jurisdiction properly belonging to the state (and other spheres .of life), thereby creating a kind of societal ecclesiocracy. However, the emergence of this state of affairs is completely understandable when viewed in historical and theological context. The early church, rooted in the scriptures, understood that the gospel had in view a *worldwide kingdom* and empire of Jesus Christ; the kingdoms of the earth were becoming the kingdoms of our Lord and of His Christ (Rev. 11:15). Moreover, in the present age, Jesus Christ is ruler of the kings of the earth (Ps. 2; Rev. 1:5). The preaching of this gospel of the kingdom was clearly for all peoples under heaven, and the nations were to be taught and discipled in obedience to everything Christ commanded (Matt. 28:16-20). Moreover, in the context of this worldwide kingdom, the church as Christ's spiritual body and called-out people was ultimately one and catholic – which simply means *universal.*

There was nothing wrong with this scriptural understanding of the *extent* of the dominion and empire of *Jesus Christ* (cf. Ps. 2; 110; Is. 42:1-9; Rev. 1:5); the problems emerge in understanding how this dominion expresses itself in the various societal institutions. As the Roman Empire broke into Eastern and Western parts, leading to the division of a Greek Orthodox and Western church, over time *imperial Rome* emerged in the foreground, dominated by a relatively undifferentiated hierarchical power structure in which church and state had become *entwined* in one another. As the Roman empire began to fail, power shifts resulted. Kuyper's description of the result is telling:

> When the *imperial* power of Rome faded, then the *ecclesiastical* influence of the bishop of Rome increased. It was inevitable that the ecclesiastical power, which continued to develop under this hierarchical presidency of the pope, became the competitor to the decaying political unity...the Roman Empire...gradually crumbled altogether.... And since the significance of the political unity of power continually diminished, it was inevitable that the ecclesiastical power – which even more strongly possessed a universal character – eventually overshadowed the political power. This could change only when the Roman Empire was transferred to the Germanic nations as the "Holy Roman Empire," but this happened by making an ever-stronger opposition between emperor and pope. The doctrine of the two swords entered the world...; the pope was to be honored as the representative of Christ, and therefore all worldly power should be subject to Rome's tribunal.[140]

This meant that in much of Europe the word of the pope became effective law.

This view of the church itself as a universally instituted power over all life was reinforced in the High and Late Middle Ages because Roman Catholic theology, as mediated through the Aristotelianism of Thomas Aquinas, regarded the church as belonging to a domain of *grace*, above and superior to *nature*.[141] This involved a strictly hierarchical view of reality and society with the church perched at the top as the gateway to eternal perfection and bliss – the state playing a support role in bringing people toward earthly moral perfection. The church's 'super-natural' theology of grace, a *donum supperadditum* (an added gift), meant that for culture to be *Christian* it had to be an *ecclesiastical* culture – that is, largely led and governed by the instituted church – upheld by the authority and ecclesiastical sanction of the pope over kings and commoners. In other words, the various spheres of life needed to be *churchified* and brought within the wide embrace of ecclesiastical authority if they were to be purified and have lasting value – especially politics. Church involvement or oversight was seen as sanctifying otherwise profane activities and spheres of life.

The church hierarchy of the Middles Ages thus became entrenched in a protracted struggle with numerous princes and emperors to control the affairs of various realms and kingdoms, sometimes even employing the power of the sword to accomplish its ends – a power that God had clearly given to the state (cf. Rom. 13:1-4), not to the institutional church. For as long as this supposedly *sacred realm* of the church (an upper storey of *grace*) held sway over a *secular realm* of nature (a lower storey of reality including the political institution of the state), a semblance of Christian society could be maintained in the form of a unified ecclesiastical culture. But with the Renaissance toward the end of the Middle Ages, the overarching authority of the church institution was steadily undermined, and the tenuous union of *nature* (reason, family, state, education, arts etc.,) and *grace* (the church with her ecclesiastical authority and theology) was shattered. The so-called realm of 'nature' no longer wanted the 'super-natural' to rule over or supervise it and the West began *secularizing.*

Along with the Renaissance came the steady rise of universities and a revival of pagan Greek thought. A concurrent spiritual decay was taking place in the church where the gospel was being increasingly obscured – both realities meant a growing resistance to an ecclesiastical domination of life. As a consequence, the church of Rome's authority steadily weakened. People began to feel that the relationship of church and state was distorted by the assertion that civil authority was *derived* in part from the bishop of Rome. The desire for renewal and reformation in church and society culminated in the sixteenth century Reformation, which split the Western church in two.

"The papist power lost its universal significance and the church, after the attempt to lord it over the state, now in turn became subject to the power of the state."[142]

The *subjection* of the church to the state proved just as problematic for the church and society in general as the subjection of the state to the church had done. Despite the Reformation, which broke emphatically with Rome, different Protestant churches sought to have themselves established as the *official church* of a given state or realm. This arrangement where the state assumes an effective leadership over the church is called *caesaropapism*.

It is well understood that under Martin Luther's leadership, since the churches in Germany needed the support of German princes to break the hierarchical power of Rome, the tendency was to *subject the church* more extensively to the state. In Lutheran domains the princes were given power not just *over* the church, but claimed a spiritual influence *within* it, receiving episcopal rank to function as leaders with Luther's agreement. The same is true in many Eastern European countries with an established state church. The Church of England established by Henry VIII also effectively broke with Rome. Here the regal head of state became the head of the church. A little later in the seventeenth century, even the evangelical Scots, negotiating with the English Parliament in conflict with Charles I, sought to have Presbyterianism established as the official state church in England and failed – in part because many of the puritans in the Cromwellian era favoured the independence of the churches. However, with the return of Charles II in 1660, a series of Acts called the Clarendon Code were eventually passed, which persecuted Protestants who were not part of the Church of England.

Despite all this, with the Calvinistic branch of the Reformation, a different view of the church's relationship to the state did begin to emerge – a theme we will return to in more detail later. It is true that these Reformed Protestant churches initially needed the military might of their rulers to resist Spain, Austria and France to prevent the destruction of Protestantism in its infancy, but the theological resources to reject the Roman view (that saw the church institute as over civil government) and the Lutheran view (that saw the state ruling over the church) were present and ready to be developed where a truly independent church influenced political life by means other than government establishment, subsidy or control. The Westminster Confession of 1647 lays out the general contours of this position: "The Lord Jesus, as King and Head of His Church, hath therein appointed a government in the hand of Church officers distinct from the civil magistrate" (chapter 30, section 1). As Greg Bahnsen points out in his detailed analysis of the Confession:

> [T]he Confession guards the separation of church and state by keeping the civil magistrate out of ecclesiastical business and jurisdiction. Moreover, the Confession protects the state from authoritative intervention or intrusive jurisdiction by the church ... The magistrate may appeal to the church for advice, or in extraordinary cases the church may out of conscience rebuke the actions of the magistrate; but the church is prohibited from meddling, handling or concluding matters which pertain solely to civil affairs. It should be noted that certain matters of public morality are not solely the concern of the commonwealth.[143]

Ever since the Enlightenment, secularization has *not* meant maintaining a jurisdictional separation of church and state – which was already maintained by the reformed confessions; contemporary secularization constitutes an effort to jettison altogether both the church *institute* and *God Himself* from all aspects of so-called 'nature' (i.e., most of everyday life, culture and politics) in order to maximize space for the 'free play' of the human personality. This has pushed the old unified ecclesiastical vision of Roman Catholicism further and further back into its own microcosm where the conflation of church and state remains most overt. In Vatican City – an independent city state enclaved within Rome (the smallest sovereign state in the world) – the state is ruled by an absolute elective monarch, the pope. Though a distinct entity, Vatican City is under the dominion and sovereign authority of the *Holy See*. The Vatican's legal system is distinct from that of Italy and the Bishop of Rome is head of state and church, exercising *ex-officio* supreme legislative, executive, and judicial power.

As already noted, however, the fault in problematic church-state relations has not solely resided with the church. Historically *the state* has regularly sought to usurp the authority and role of the church. We have seen that with *caesaropapism* in both East and West, it was often civil governments and states that, for political purposes, wanted the official establishment of particular churches so that they could be controlled, manipulated, or put to political purpose. Because of the established Church in England, even today, the British Prime Minister is required to play an important role in the selection of the Archbishop of Canterbury which, since they are political appointees, has significant implications for the English church. Due in part to their positions of political power and state support, compromised or faithless bishops often play the role of chaplains to the secular state in the House of Lords, rubber-stamping the progressive drift rather than standing faithfully for the truth of the gospel. The British monarch is also Head of the Church of England and *Defensor fidei* (defender of the faith), but this has meant little or nothing in recent decades to arrest decline and decay in the establishment.

Despite its many faults, at least in this system the Church of England has been historically regarded as something important and unique in society, functioning in the past as a conscience for the nation and could expect a certain amount of respect, protection and recognition from civil government. However, in the Erastian collegial system which obtains in places like the Netherlands, there is no material difference between a church, a mosque, a Buddhist temple, a synagogue, or a sports club. They are simply regarded by the state as various 'societies' which government must ensure will respect civil law and not hinder individual freedom. There is no recognition in civil government that God is at work in a special way in the life and witness of Christian churches, nor do they enjoy a unique independence that would distinguish them from a soccer club or a society of Jedi knights. Churches have gradually become 'societies' to be controlled and managed by the 'neutral' state. Abraham Kuyper opined:

> Caesaropapism assumes power over the church, and then the church turns to stone. If the modern state denies the autonomous character and higher right of Christ's church, then the church degenerates into the status of a society or an entirely ordinary association.[144]

At the more extreme end of state interference and control, in various dictatorships of the modern era, the church has been grossly assaulted, used and manipulated. In Nazi Germany for example, Hitler sought to seize control of the national church and use it to further his own messianic claims. The German Evangelical Church in the grip of caesaropapism had a long and misguided tradition of subservient loyalty to the state. In the 1920s, a movement emerged within this church called the "German Christians" (*Deutsche Christen*). Under the influence of the Nazi state in the 1930s, these people embraced many aspects of Nazi thinking and sought the creation of a national "Reich Church" which promoted a nazified version of Christianity. In opposition to the "German Christians" a "Confessing Church" (*Bekennende Kirche*) emerged. Their *Barmen Declaration* asserted that the church's allegiance was to God and Scripture and not to any earthly *Führer*. The German Evangelical church was thus divided and a struggle within German Protestantism ensued. Many of the Confessing Church leaders were persecuted, betrayed, imprisoned or executed.

Historian Frank Dikotter notes the religiously tinged claims of various twentieth century dictators:

> Hitler presented himself as a messiah united with the masses in a mystical, quasi-religious bond. Mussolini encouraged feelings of devotion and worship characteristic of Christian piety. There were holy sites, holy pictures, pilgrimages, the hope of a healing touch from the leader. In the Soviet Union, even as the Orthodox Church came under siege, a new religion under the red star appeared, with a corner dedicated to Lenin in factories, offices, restaurants, some of them real altars decorated with ribbons and wreaths. [145]

Conflict, confusion and usurpation as well as manipulation, impersonation and control have thus been commonplace in the history of the West in the relation of church and state – each seeking supremacy over the other at different times and in various circumstances. As Christian faith has declined in influence, Western society has sought to renegotiate its relationship to the church (secularization) and reinterpret its remarkable and enduring Christian history, largely by condemning its own past. At the same time, believers have been left wondering how to understand the role of the church in the current socio-political environment.

What is the Church?

To begin to resolve the church-state-society problem, a close look at the nature of the church is required. In view of the fact that religion is basic to all of life (whether Christian, Islamic, pagan, humanistic etc.,) and that the inescapable condition of faith within human existence touches all the areas of our experience in the world, many Christians *intuitively* recognize that Christianity must be a faith *for all of life*. That is, they recognize that Christ's claims about Himself, His kingdom and people must be deeply significant beyond their own personal devotion since they appear all-encompassing and universal. However, difficulties arise in considering the way these claims *apply* to His called-out people, *the church*, in their societal relationships.

It is these questions surrounding the concrete *application* of Christ's claims which occasion confusion as to the character and calling of the church and how it should relate to the state and other social entities and institutions. For example, should the church *institute* assert itself and its beliefs over other social entities and institutions as the *primary agent* of the kingdom, or are the kingdom of God and the church institute basically identical so that Christ's sovereign reign need only be manifest in the life of the gathered church congregation? Alternatively, is the reality of Christ's kingdom to shape all of life and culture with the church institute as one of many expressions of that reality? To address this, we need to begin by briefly asking ourselves what the church *is*, and what the church is meant to *do*. This will allow us to consider the relationship of the church and the kingdom of God, and then to define an ideal relationship of the church institute to the state and other societal institutions.

In the scriptures, Christ promises to *build His church* (Matt. 16:18). The Greek term for church is *ekklesia* and is rendered from the Hebrew *Qahal* and *Edah,* which were used as the standing names for the *congregation* of Israel. The church is therefore a called out and gathered people united into one community by the preaching of the gospel. This people, both Jew and Gentile (Eph. 2), are those that recognize Jesus as Lord, king and messiah and inherit the promises forfeited by the old faithless congregation of Israel. Among this new people are manifest the powers of the world to come. Willem Ouweneel correctly identifies five different senses or meanings of the Christian church found in the New Testament. First, we observe a worldwide, transcendent, *invisible church* which is the *body of Christ*, transcending any temporal period, from its origin to the second coming (Eph. 3:9-11; 5:23-24, 32). Second, we can identify a worldwide, *immanent-historical church* (Eph. 2:21; Col. 2:19), which is the *visible church* here on earth that through development and growth, ruin and renewal, traverses a certain history. It comprises all true believers, spread over the whole earth, in all times and places. Third, we have the *worldwide concretely actual church* – the totality of believers at this given moment who are here on earth (Gal. 1:13). Then we can also speak of the *local church*, which is the totality of believers in a city, town or village (Acts 8:1; 13:1; 15:4; Rom. 16:1; Rev. 2-3). In this sense the Greek *ekklesia* can also be used in the plural (1 Cor. 16:1; 2 Cor. 8:1; Rev. 1:4) and can refer to the *meeting* of the local churches (1 Cor. 11:18; Eph. 3:21; Col. 4:16). Finally, we can speak of the *church as a part of the local church* that may meet in various places like the home (Acts 5:14; 12:12; Rom. 16:3-5).[146]

In much modern usage, the worldwide, transcendent element of the invisible body is typically overlooked. People tend to speak of the church as a *building* or as having a regional meaning like the Church of England or the Evangelical (Lutheran) Church of Germany. We tend not to think as much as we should in the broader terms of Scripture's view of the church. In addition, many denominations have arisen in the course of history which consist of various geographically *local congregations* – more or less formally organized within a given hierarchy or administration. So, when people speak of the *Church of England* for example, or the *Fellowship of Evangelical Baptists in Ontario*, we encounter a different meaning of "church" to any of the five mentioned in the Bible. This historical development is not itself wrong, but is important to note because, when we speak of "the church" teaching, evangelizing, engaging the community or doing various other things, we do not mean the invisible universal body of Christ, or the immanent-historical visible church as a whole, but rather this or that locally instituted congregation or denomination. Moreover, in a strict sense, "the church" doesn't teach or evangelize or discipline; different teachers and leaders within local congregations or denominations teach and evangelize, with elders and pastors being the ones who discipline.

So, what authority and jurisdiction does the *local church institute* have apart from singing, praying, preaching and prophesying, evangelizing, disciplining members and celebrating the Lord's Supper? Ouweneel points out:

> [T]his authority applies at most to itself, its own members, and this through its elders. There is no such thing in the Bible as "the" church exercising authority over other societal relationships, over families, over society, even over the state…; this is pure scholasticism, a certain Protestant denomination now usurping the position that the Roman Catholic Church had during the Middle Ages…. As an immanent community of people, an association with rulers and regulations, church councils and church fees, every church denomination is, from a purely *structural* point of view, a societal relationship like any other.[147]

It would make no sense to suggest, for example, that the *universal church* has authority over certain areas of a Christian's life – how could that ever be applied meaningfully? It is only local elders who have a limited authority over the believer in the life of the local church.

Why is this important and does this evaluation somehow undermine the importance of the Christian church and its authority? Firstly, there is nothing in this analysis that minimizes the critical importance and significance of the gathered congregation of believers in local churches for worship, prayer, preaching, the sacraments, and the privilege of church discipline. What it shows, however, is that we cannot transfer the significance, jurisdiction or authority of Christ's universal-transcendent body and kingdom reign to the life of any local and historically realized congregation or denomination. Nor can we turn any instituted expression of the church of Christ into "the" church that is now exercising this or that power and authority *over* other spheres of life. It is Christ alone who exercises power and authority through believers *in all spheres* of life. As Ouweneel shows:

> In living my Christian life, my marriage, my family, my local congregation, and even my Christian schools and associations, are equally important as autonomous expressions of the one kingdom of God. In each of these societal relationships, I am under the Lordship of Christ. As such my membership of the local congregation is not more important than my being a Christian husband, parent, professor, businessman, and party member...; *the kingdom of God on earth encompasses all these societal associations.*[148]

If this were not so, one's relationship to the local church congregation would be elevated over all other supposedly "common institutions," (like marriage, family or vocation) just as "grace" is supposedly elevated over "nature" in all expressions of scholastic philosophy and theology. To be clear, what is *not* being said here is that being a businessman or husband will last forever. The local Christian school my children attend is not an everlasting reality like being a member of the invisible, transcendent body of Christ. However, my local church or even denomination is constantly changing in various ways and will not last forever either. Locally instituted churches are not permanent – just consider the warnings historically fulfilled against the churches in the book of Revelation.

With what can be a startling realization that the role of the church is relativized in its place in terms of the kingdom of God, it is sometimes objected that the scriptures are addressed to 'the church,' marking the church *institute* out as higher or prior in importance to all other areas of life. But this would be at best a half truth. The Older Testament is not addressed to the church as instituted by the Lord through the disciples, but to all God's people throughout all of history. Moreover, some of it is clearly directed at the unbelieving pagan world, like several of the prophecies of Amos. The Bible reveals that the Word of God comes to all kinds of men and nations, in all kinds of places, to both believers and unbelievers, Jews and Gentiles.

It is true of course that the apostle Paul did not write letters that we know of to Christian schools, political parties or companies (there probably weren't any at the time), but he did address letters to churches (plural). More often, however, his letters are addressed to Christians as saints, that is to groups of Christians (Rom. 1:7; Eph. 1:1; Phil. 1:1; Col. 1:2) and also to individual Christians like Timothy, Titus and Philemon. Only when writing to the Corinthians and Thessalonians are *churches* addressed explicitly. The other letters are addressed simply to Christians, "and as such they are not only church members, but also Christian husbands and wives, Christian parents and children, Christian employers and employees (Eph. 5:22-6:9; Col. 3:18-4:1; 1 Pet. 3:1-7)."[149]

I have taken space to emphasize the importance of distinguishing properly what we mean when speaking about "the church" because if we go astray here, the consequences are far-reaching for cultural and political life. The implication of what I am arguing here is that my local congregation or denomination, if faithful to an orthodox Christian confession, important as it is, is only one small, temporal and visible expression of the universal, transcendent and invisible body over which Christ Himself is absolute head. There can be no question that, as Geerhardus Vos notes, "the kingdom-forces which are at work, the kingdom-life which exists in the invisible sphere, find expression in the kingdom-organism of the visible church."[150] There is mighty kingdom power at work in Christ's instituted church that cannot be ignored, bypassed or minimized in the Christian life. In addition, the authority exercised in faithful churches derives from Christ, not men. However, from this it does *not* follow, as Vos recognizes, that "the visible church is the only outward expression of the visible kingdom."[151] To borrow a biological metaphor, we can think of the church as *organism* – the universal *body* of Christ consisting of all believers serving Christ as Lord in *all of life* – and of the locally *instituted* church which includes the specific organization and tasks of church elders, pastors and the various offices as well as the obligations of members of the congregation to each other. This called-out people are then given the task of going out into all the world with both the message and reconciling life of the kingdom of God in the power of the Holy Spirit.

The Church and the Kingdom

This more precise description of the church highlights both the intimate *relation* as well as the vital *distinction* between the church and the kingdom of God. Vos notes that "the conception of the kingdom is common to all periods of our Lord's teaching, that of the church emerges only at two special points of His ministry as recorded in Matthew 16:18 and 18:17."[152] The word for 'Kingdom' in the New Testament is *basileia*. It is the significance and power of this now manifest reality, first organized amongst the disciples by the Lord, that the gospel as a whole has in view. Although occasionally the concepts of the kingdom and the church seem almost parallel (because of their intimate relation), Herman Ridderbos in his classic work *The Coming of the Kingdom* notes:

> [W]e should point out that the concept *basileia* nowhere occurs in the sense of this idea of the *ekklesia*. Nor is it used in the sense that the kingdom of God in its provisional manifestation on earth would be embodied in the form and organization of the church...; by the term kingdom of God we can denote not

only the fulfilling and completing action of God in relation to the entire cosmos, but also various facets of this all-embracing process. Thus, e.g., the territory within which this divine action occurs and in which the blessings of the kingdom are enjoyed is called the *basileia* of God or that of heaven (cf. Matt. 5:20; 11:11; 23:13).[153]

Clearly, the scriptural teaching about being *in* the kingdom of God or *entering* the kingdom of God as a fulfilled reality through Christ is not describing a person's admittance into a temporal, local Christian community. The Bible simply does not use *basileia* in the sense of "church," yet it never minimizes the importance of the church as the new people on mission within the revelation of Christ and His kingdom. The setting aside of empirical Israel as the covenant people and the formation of a new humanity as the seed of Abraham and children of the kingdom is realized in the coming of Christ and is explicitly taught by Him: "Therefore say I unto you, the *kingdom* of God shall be taken from you, and given to a *nation* (people) bringing forth the fruits thereof" (Matt. 21:43-46). In short, the salvation of the kingdom is being given to a new people to be gathered in by the Messiah. In this context we find *both* concepts, of the kingdom and a new people of God. This called-out people will manifest and bring forth the *fruits of the kingdom*. Church and kingdom therefore are *not* identical. Ridderbos is incisive:

> The *basileia* is the great divine work of salvation in its fulfilment and consummation in Christ; the *ekklesia* is the people elected and called by God and sharing in the bliss of the *basileia*. Logically the *basileia* ranks first, and not the *ekklesia*. The former, therefore, has a much more comprehensive content. It represents the all-embracing perspective, it denotes the consummation of all history, brings both grace and judgment, has cosmic dimensions, fills time and eternity. The *ekklesia* in all this is the people who in this great drama have been placed

on the side of God in Christ by virtue of the divine election and covenant. They have been given the divine promise, have been brought to manifestation and gathered together by the preaching of the gospel, and will inherit the redemption of the kingdom now and in the great future.[154]

The gathered church remains critical in all of this because "the *ekklesia* is the fruit of the revelation of the *basileia*; and conversely, the *basileia* is inconceivable without the *ekklesia*. The one is inseparable from the other without, however, the one merging into the other."[155] The church then is to be constantly moved, motivated and inspired by the reality that as God's people, the body of Christ, we are chosen instruments of the *basileia* in teaching God's commandments, preaching and applying God's Word to our lives, living out in all its fullness the kingdom charter revealed in Scripture – a charter which demands all things be reconciled to God in Christ (2 Cor. 5:19).

The clear distinction and relation of the church and kingdom of God helps us to recognize several important things. *First,* it enables us to appreciate and value the important role the church has in its own God-ordained sphere and to be committed to its local visible expression. Here we worship together, are taught the Word, receive the sacraments, enjoy faithful discipline and care for one another in an accountable community with other believers. *Second,* it helps us to see that the calling of the Christian believer is much bigger and more comprehensive in scope than participation in the instituted church as a worshipping community. A kingdom vision frees us from misguided ecclesiastical domination and liberates the believer's *entire life in all its aspects,* to be concretely subject to the Lordship of Jesus Christ and His Word – making the totality of the Christian's life in all spheres an instrument of the kingdom of God. As Vos writes:

> [The] kingship of God, as his recognized and applied supremacy, is intended to pervade and control *the whole of human life in all*

its forms of existence. This the parable of the leaven plainly teaches. These various forms of human life have each their own sphere in which they work and embody themselves. There is a sphere of science, a sphere of art, a sphere of the family and of the state, a sphere of commerce and industry. Whenever one of these spheres comes under the controlling influence of the principle of the divine supremacy and glory, and this outwardly reveals itself, there we can truly say that the kingdom of God has become manifest.[156]

The detailed application of this is the calling of every believer – that every province of human life and thought be brought under the sway of God's kingdom. Yet critically, as Vos notes, "it was not [Christ's] intention that this result should be reached by making human life in all its spheres subject to the visible church."[157]

The Proper Relation of Church, State, and Society

This brings us to our final argument concerning the way in which kingdom life works itself out and the role the church plays in relation to other spheres of life. With the *basileia/ekklesia* distinction in place we can now see more clearly the various errors in regard to the relationship of church and state. I began this chapter by noting a false dilemma that is typically present in modern evangelical thinking regarding Christianity and political life: pursue a return to an ecclesiastical cultural model with a formally or informally established church taking charge in various aspects of cultural and political life, or acknowledge the secular state as the new unifying principle. I have implied that there is in fact a third option implicit in a proper understanding of the nature of the church and the kingdom of God which avoids the false problematics engendering the struggle between these polarizing views.

On this fresh understanding it becomes clear that relating the gospel (Christianity) to the various aspects of society *does not* require relating the *church institute,* its offices and functions, directly or indirectly to everything possible in society – the first position within the false dilemma I have highlighted is thus exposed as in error. The idea that one needs to *churchify* life to express the life of the kingdom of God – the general assumption that Christianizing culture would require churchmen in high political positions, running schools and universities, governing hospitals and charities, and in one way or another inserting the church's offices and functions into as many areas of life as possible is in reality a hangover from the scholastic thought of the medieval era and the ecclesiastical culture of old Christendom.

Historically, as the church's former influence in this regard steadily waned after the Renaissance, more and more spheres of life were being differentiated and appreciated in Western society, like schools and universities, the arts and sciences, clubs and associations etc., The Roman Catholic Church's (scholastic) solution to recognizing these various societal spheres as having a degree of independence, while retaining an ecclesiastical cultural vision, was to posit the principle of *subsidiarity.* Here, a *relative autonomy* is given to various subordinate areas of life while being conceived as parts within the all-encompassing whole of the *state.* However, this *natural* state is in turn *superseded* and shaped by the church as a *supernatural* institute of grace. The idea was introduced into Catholic social teaching by Bishop Wilhelm Emmanuel von Ketteler of Mainz in the 1850s but was built on an earlier Thomistic understanding of life.[158] Aquinas had viewed the state as the all-inclusive total community in the realm of *nature,* embracing all other spheres of societal life in a whole-parts relation. Of course, the state's jurisdiction did not extend to the church as a *supernatural* domain of grace – the state was only the *portal* to that domain under the church's supervision.

In this model, the family is at the bottom of a *hierarchy* of communities that culminates in the state, supervised and spiritually overseen by the church. This hierarchical structure is the core principle of *subsidiarity*. This basically pagan view does not recognize or appreciate the *unique character* of the various social spheres of life as ordained by God. There is a vague conception of the 'common good' to be pursued by the state, but no *criterion* for achieving this. Thomism and Romanism certainly do not want to openly embrace state absolutism, but the societal doctrine of subsidiarity provides no theoretical defense against it. As Herman Dooyeweerd explains, the Roman error was locating the necessarily Christian character of a just state in the control of the church institute:

> Its Christian character was not Scripturally sought in the expression of Christ's Kingdom within the inner structure of the state itself, but Roman Catholicism continued to see the inner structure of the state in the old pagan way as the total bond of all natural society, and continued to deduce the principles for political life by 'natural reason' apart from revelation. The state can participate in the realm of grace, not from within but, since it is itself strictly natural, it can do this only by enlisting in the service of the temporal church-institute.[159]

The attempt of the Roman Church to hold together church and state in ecclesiastical union by making the state the all-encompassing *natural* institution, supervised by the church as a *super-natural* one, cannot be justified scripturally and its historic record in providing religious liberty is poor. Yet a version of it has been incorporated into much of modern evangelical thinking. In this evangelical version, the state and socio-cultural life are essentially disconnected not only from the church institute, but from God's rule, His Word and His redemptive work altogether, and allowed to go their own way. Ultimately, the principle of subsidiarity is a violation of both a creational and scriptural principal because, "the state does not *grant existence* to any non-state sphere sovereign social entity. It merely has to acknowledge that, on equal footing, there are multiple distinct and sphere sovereign societal entities."[160]

These Romanist and evangelical variations on a theme fail to properly distinguish the church and the kingdom of God, viewing the church as the principal or only agent of that kingdom. However, as we have seen, since the church cannot be conflated with the kingdom of God itself, the instituted historical church (of whichever tradition) does *not* have the burden of imposing its confession or authority on the state or the rest of society – it does not need to control or ecclesiasticize society by bringing it under its control. The unique spheres of family, state, academy, business etc., are *not* the church, nor are they subordinate *parts* of the church. Critically however, this does *not* mean they are not to be Christian, transformed and shaped by the gospel, the Word of God and Lordship of Christ. It only means they are not required to be under ecclesiastical control. When it comes to political life and society, the church's role is to prophetically *propose*, not *impose* its biblical insight for culture.

With regard to the opposite pole in our false dilemma, the tragic knee-jerk reaction of much contemporary evangelicalism to secularization has not been to try and impose its religious confession on political life, but to erroneously assume a need to dissolve *any relationship* between Christianity, political life and the broader culture. This is done by implicitly or explicitly devaluing creation and culture as a lower or lesser domain of reality and then essentially collapsing the church and the kingdom of God into one another – often identified as a special domain of grace or 'redemptive kingdom.' In rightly recognizing the need to separate church and state in terms of jurisdiction and function, they have effectively separated God, His kingdom and His Law-Word from human cultural activity and the exercise of power and authority in the public sphere. Many of the intellectuals sympathetic to this response end up adopting and promoting individualistic and progressive liberal *democracy* as the most suitable political philosophy for preserving freedoms and a minimal right to preach the gospel – a hope collapsing before our eyes in the West. This untenable liberal position tries to hold together two intractably conflicting principles: a radical autonomy of the individual will (the *right* to sin against God and be a law unto oneself) on the one hand, and the Christian notion of a transcendent moral law and authority on the other. The result has been the flourishing of a naked pagan individualism alongside a sceptical subjectivism. These ideas find institutional expression in a supposedly 'neutral' secular state. Not only is such a state anything but religiously neutral, it gradually undermines all social order and defeats its own purportedly democratic purpose. As K. L. Grasso points out:

> Contemporary liberalism subverts the foundations of democratic government because the thoroughgoing subjectivism towards which liberalism inexorably tends precludes in principle an affirmation of an objective and universally obligatory order of justice and rights, and the dignity of the human person. The resultant culture of unbridled individualism and subjectivism is scarcely a fertile soil for the cultivation of republican virtues on which democracy depends.[161]

The attempt of so many Christians today to locate in secular liberal democracy a 'Christian' solution to the relationship of faith and culture, Christianity and the state, must be understood in its broader historical context of the false dilemma already highlighted. On the one hand there is fear of a return to the darker days of religious persecution if a distinctly Christian state and political vision is pursued. On the other hand, self-preservation amidst a radical and aggressive re-paganization of culture motivates the desire to adopt a form of public religious and even legal pluralism that would ostensibly allow Christians to 'remain at the table.' In other cases, secular liberal democracy is chosen simply for want of awareness or understanding of a better and authentically scriptural alternative to the unified ecclesiastical culture of former Christendom and the radical cultural and political relativization of the claims of Christ in modern socialistic liberal democracies.

Because in both cases modern Christians mistakenly see the kingdom of God and the church as functionally the same, and because we rightly recognize that not everyone is 'saved' and should not be coerced into being part of the visible church, we have tended to assume that a truly Christian order for political life is rendered inherently impossible unless a given church with its peculiar confession controls and coerces people to think and act 'Christianly.' Since this is obviously unacceptable, the Christianization of culture, including political life, is rejected as unChristian! It is here that we meet the need for a clearly articulated and scripturally grounded Christian political vision that avoids the pitfall of ecclesiastical coercion and domination whilst rejecting the ideological myth of religious neutrality in politics.

Chapter 6

STATE ABSOLUTISM, SPHERE SOVEREIGNTY AND THE LIMITS OF POLITICAL AUTHORITY

State Absolutism

One of the most remarkable features of the late modern era has been the strange coalescence of an incessant call for 'total emancipation' from the shackles of alleged oppression with an explicit totalitarian drift in political life. This initially seems contradictory. On one side there is an anarchistic demand for human life and activity, but it is tied to a totalitarian tendency which, in the name of freedom and radical democracy, allows civil government to pursue its task without any *intrinsic limitations*. This perplexing element of life in the West manifests itself in a constant clamouring amongst the people for complete self-determination, equality and self-expression in the name of 'justice,' whilst looking to the state as the appropriate organ to legislate the rights, entitlements and freedoms being demanded into existence. People increasingly require total equality, provision, safety and security to be delivered by the state, and it is taken practically for granted that the central government must act as the lord and coordinator of all society. The reformed philosopher Jan Dengerink is to the point:

> To [central government] is ascribed a clear supremacy over all
> other basically non-political groups. In this fashion, we land up

squarely, under the banner of absolute freedom and equality, with a typical totalitarian conception of the state. This clearly shows its out-workings in the socio-political activities of various Western democracies, with all of the structural and spiritual leveling that follows from it ... the result is always a heavy-handed bureaucracy, which in practice reduces the individual citizen to a nullity, one in which the technocrats and social planners get the final say ...[162]

This political reality can be identified as a form of liberal democratic socialism and it trends totalitarian: "Abolishing in principle the unique, original responsibility of all kinds of other societal structures, it hands society over to the all-devouring state leviathan."[163] Put differently, the majority of people have become *statist* in their thinking, implicitly or explicitly. The central meaning of statism is important to note. The presence of an '-*ism*' should immediately alert the careful thinker to the possibility that there has been an exaggeration of a created and God-ordained structure (in this case the state) into something well beyond its intended function. Fundamentally statism is a political system in which the sphere of civil government exerts substantial, centralized control over much of society, including the economy and various other spheres.

The dominance of statism today means that few people question anymore progressive, redistributive taxation (including inheritance taxes), national minimum wage laws, market interventionism, the suspension of civil liberties by unelected bureaucrats in the name of public health, banking and big corporation bailouts, state control and funding of medicine, education, charity (through various regulations and incentives) and welfare, as well as a large share of the media such as the BBC and CBC. The British National Health Service alone is one of the world's largest employers.[164] The public sector has become so vast that most people have grown accustomed to the state's omnipresence. Britain today is not a country that the famed British Prime Minister Winston Churchill would have imagined emerging from a conflict *against* state absolutism.

In this brave new world, the church herself is increasingly treated as little more than another social club with no more significance in culture than a cinema or sports team – possibly less. It is easy to forget the fact that there is in our era a *regulated* state-church in officially communist countries like China, where some of the churches are authorised by the civil government to gather, worship, practice the rites of the church and even preach from (parts of) the Bible. However, the apparent 'liberties' of those state-approved churches are emphatically constrained by government, including subjects they can address from Scripture. They must submit themselves unequivocally to every regulation, *recognizing state authority as absolute.* It has only been because of faithful pastors and leaders in China standing on the full authority of the Word of God and the sovereignty of Christ the King, that an 'underground' church which refuses to recognize state control over it, has grown. Yet in the West we seem increasingly ready to allow the state to licence, control and regulate the churches, even to the point of locking them down indefinitely and at will if 'public health' functionaries of the state require it, and ceasing pastoral counseling in biblical truth for those struggling with their sexuality.

The explosion of the *regulatory state* in the last 70 years, and especially over the last 30, reaching into more and more areas of private life and civil society, is rooted in the idea of the *omni-competence* of the state and its bureaucracy. Neither Scripture nor Christian historical thought well into the early twentieth century ever envisions such a freedom-sapping behemoth overtaking life. Today, there is no end to the tens of thousands of state regulations to be obeyed in the anglosphere in numerous departments of life. As I found out after a recent move, there are permits required for almost every kind of renovation activity on private property (including the size and colour of garden sheds or moving a bathroom sink) as well as detailed regulations covering the uses of one's property. There are permits and regulations for working from a home office, as well as onerous worksite and office regulations. In fact, the regulations in Western nations are so diverse they cover everything from the size and shape of bananas, the length of nails required in drywall and who is allowed to feed pigs. More regulations require permits for collecting rags and metal, and others control games on private premises. Various bylaws mandate the number of parking spaces required per seat in church sanctuaries (Toronto) and liquor stores are barred from selling refrigerated water or soda (Indiana). The list is literally endless and frequently absurd.

This 'omni-competent' vision of the state has become so ubiquitous that many evangelical Christians have lost their cultural memory of God-given, *pre-political* institutions, rights and responsibilities that are to be protected, but are not *created*, *controlled* or *governed* by the state. As a consequence, believers have floundered in their response to unprecedented and illegal lockdowns of the church, the growing collapse of civil liberties, the total control of education, expanded abortion, euthanasia, no-fault divorce law, the redefinition of marriage and family, homosexuality and transgender issues, largely because a *scriptural world and life view* norming our understanding of these questions and the role of the state with respect to them has collapsed. Instead, we have a liberal democratic and statist worldview drilled into us by the various organs of cultural life, where Jesus and a hope of heaven is spread on top as a sort of spiritual condiment giving religious flavor to secularism via the ministry of the churches.

What has become increasingly clear in recent decades is that we are entering an era (likely protracted) of struggle for the freedom of the church in the West, not just with the state and its bureaucracy, but with various church movements themselves, some of whose leaders are emerging as committed apologists for statism. There has never been a shortage of cultural leaders ready to support and advise falling down before the image of the absolutist state when the music plays – to obey the state elites without question. It is always the Daniels and his three friends ready to pray despite the king's edict, or refusing to bow down to overreaching political power, who are in short supply. As a result, when it comes to analysing threats to freedom from their own civil government, courts and bureaucracy, Christians are generally poorly equipped. Like the proverbial frog slowly boiled to death for failing to detect the rising temperature of the water, we are sleepwalking toward tyranny.

The Sovereignty of God

This state of affairs is not just a problem; it is a tragedy, because it is the abandonment of the *legacy of the reformation* which gradually gave us both the free English national church and eventually liberty for non-conformity (Toleration Act, 1689), giving shape to the political life of the entire anglosphere. Abraham Kuyper, an heir of the same reformed tradition on the continent of Europe and who for a time served as Prime Minister of the Netherlands – a country with one of the richest legacies of Christian freedom from the time of William of Orange[165] – has pointed out that:

> The dominating principle [of the Calvinistic side of the reformation] was not, soteriologically, justification by faith, but in the widest sense cosmologically, the *Sovereignty of the Triune God over the whole Cosmos, in all its spheres and kingdoms,* visible and invisible.[166]

This meant emphatically that the state, as well as the church, is ordained of God and under His authority as His servant (Prov. 8:15-16; Rom. 13:1ff). In Romans 13, Paul specifically and explicitly places *all authority* under God – including civil government – as a sphere of power and authority instituted by Him alone. The apostle's prescription concerning the state's task as well as his exhortation against resisting God's order in temporal authority, assumes that to do so resists *God's command* and so he presupposes the *absolute sovereignty of God*.

What is clearly at issue for Paul in Romans 13 is man's propensity to resist God's ordinances and commands. Clearly, we cannot selectively obey God's commands at our convenience – including recognizing the legitimacy of temporal authority. *All* God's commands and ordinances need to be considered and obeyed. This being the case, if the state presumes to forbid what God commands, or commands what God forbids, the state has moved beyond its delimited authority and those who obey God must at that point resist such arrogant presumption. This is clear in the chapter as Paul goes on to teach that the civil authority is God's servant – which literally means God's *deacon*. The apostle explains that this entails being a terror to bad conduct and approving of good conduct, bearing the sword to avenge those that do wrong. But if the state becomes a terror to those who do good and rewards those who do evil, it is again in flagrant violation of God's command and ordinance, and Christians have at that point a duty to resist an authority that has ceased to be God's deacon. This explains why Paul spent so much time in prison and in the courts himself because he was deemed to be resisting authority. Were this not the case, we would be bound to state absolutism with no basis for resistance to tyranny of any and every kind. So, we are to obey God's ordinance to submit to civil authorities and fulfil our obligations until the state moves against God's norms and ordinances. In all other cases we obey for the sake of our conscience and to avoid unnecessary punishment.

For centuries this had been the dominant Christian view. As James Willson wrote in his outstanding commentary on Romans 13 in 1853, nothing can nullify the law of God: "To the best government, obedience can be yielded only in things lawful; for there is a "higher law" to which rulers and subjects are alike amenable. "The heavens do rule." There is a God above us, and "to Him every knee shall bow, and every tongue shall confess that Jesus Christ is Lord, to the glory of God the Father."[167] Willson shows in great detail how Paul demonstrates that "God alone is the source of legitimate authority. He is sovereign. Man is His. Power, not derived from God is ever illegitimate. It is mere usurpation."[168] In particular, Willson is diligent to expose the misuse of Romans 13 as a text promoting passive obedience and non-resistance in the face of evil and rebellion against God:

> Paul did not intend by the language before us, to forbid even the forcible resistance of unjust and tyrannical civil magistrates, not even when that resistance is made with the avowed design of displacing offending rulers, or, it may be, the change of the very form of government itself...That question was settled in England by the revolution of 1688, when the nation, rising in its might, expelled James II as an enemy to the constitutional rights and liberties of the people. The separate national and independent existence of these United States is the fruit of successful revolution.[169]

In 1 Timothy 2:1-2, Christians are also urged by the apostle Paul to pray and intercede for kings and those in authority. Contrary to implying some sort of unquestioning subservience, this command reveals the *high mediatorial position* of the believer and Christ's instituted church. The believer is required to go to the sovereign ruler of the kings of the earth (Rev. 1:5), because of our status as a royal priesthood and holy nation before God (1 Pt. 2:9) and intercede for mercy and wisdom (or indeed judgment) to be upon earthly rulers, in order that God's people be left in peace and freedom to live godly lives. In short, believers are to use their high position before the Lord so that they can be *left alone by civil authorities*, to serve the kingdom of God.

This perspective on God's sovereignty constitutes the root of religious liberty, freedom of conscience and indeed true *political liberty* in the West. From the Christian standpoint, there is no *absolute* power or authority for Parliament, civil governments or monarchs. All authority is delegated, limited and under God in the various God-ordained spheres of life. In light of this, and because of the legitimate sword power given to the state, Kuyper rightly warns, *"we must ever watch against the danger which lurks, for our personal liberty, in the power of the state."*[170] And he keeps the state in check by likewise asserting the absolute authority of God alone:

> From the ends of the earth God cites all nations and peoples before His high judgment seat. For God created the nations. They exist for Him. They are His own. And therefore, all these nations, and in them humanity, must exist for His glory and consequently after His ordinances, in order that in their well-being, when they walk after His ordinances, His divine wisdom may shine forth ... this right is possessed by God, and by Him alone. No man has the right to rule over another man, otherwise such a right necessarily and immediately becomes the right of the strongest ... nor can a group of men, by contract, from their own right, compel you to obey a fellow man ... authority over men cannot arise from men. Just as little from a majority over against a minority.[171]

To say the least, this is not the prevailing view among professing Christians today. The spirit of the French Revolution and German philosophical pantheism permeating the West's social democracies opposes God and recognizes no ground for a just state or political authority in anything other than man himself. *"No God, no master"* was a matter of confession for the

French revolutionaries. On this view, all power and authority proceeds from man alone. Thus, the *absolute* sovereignty of the people or the state is confessional and practical atheism. This is not what the English constitutional arrangements had in mind with the idea of the sovereignty of Parliament, since it is the monarch's Parliament, and elected leaders are *invited* by the monarch to form a government. The Head of State of the United Kingdom and Canada swears an oath, under the absolute sovereignty of Christ the King, to uphold the law and gospel of Christ and to defend that faith once for all delivered to the saints. State omnipotence then, is the opposite of biblical teaching (Dan. 2:21-24; Acts 17:7) and runs contrary to the history of the English Revolution and the legacy of the mother of all parliaments. On Oliver Cromwell's tomb at Westminster Abbey, we read the epitaph (the battle cry of the Puritans), *"Christ not man is King."*

Sphere Sovereignty

It is evident then that a scripturally rooted solution is required that addresses head-on the present crisis of social order and the relationship of Christianity to political and cultural life that doesn't fall into the false dilemma dealt with in the previous chapter – a choice between a unified ecclesiastical culture and a totally relativized place for the claims of Christ and His church in a secularized order. Any solution will be inadequate if it merely *appreciates* and respects the historic separation of the jurisdictions of church and state. It must realize that *all spheres of life* – family, church, state, academy, professional associations and bodies, economic life and business, art, science, and all else besides – are themselves, in their own spheres, to be made subject to the Lordship of Christ and the Word of God, as equally important aspects of the *kingdom of God*. This creational and kingdom principle (Gen 1:28-31; 1 Cor 10:26, 31; Col 3:17) is the polar opposite of the pagan notion of the *total state* and the syncretistic idea of *subsidiarity* which seeks to Christianize the pagan ideal. As Dooyeweerd has explained:

> Neither marriage, nor family, nor blood-relation, nor the free types of social existence, whether they are organized or not, can be considered as *part* of an all-embracing state. Every societal relationship has received from God its own structure and law of life, sovereign in its own sphere. The Christian world and life view, illumined by the revealed Word of God, posits sphere sovereignty of the temporal life spheres over against the pagan totality idea.[172]

The basic creational principle at work here (Col. 1:15-20; Rev. 1:5) was first called *sphere sovereignty* by Abraham Kuyper. The fundamental teaching of sphere sovereignty rests on four essential biblical principles. The first, as already discussed, is the total sovereignty of God over all of creation which He called into existence (Ps. 103:19; Prov. 16:4). Because of the providence of God active at every moment, He also guides the development or becoming of His creation in the unfolding of its potentiality. · As such, His sovereign providence is a constant and absolute (Job 1:21; Ps. 75:6-7; Prov. 3:6; Dan 4:35; Matt. 10:29; Acts 17:26; Rom. 11:36). No area of life is exempt from the authority of the creator and redeemer (1 Chron. 29:11).

Secondly, all social institutions in their historical disclosure, despite the distortions and disturbance present due to the fall into sin, find their ultimate origin in creation since everything was separated and distinguished 'after its kind' in creation, having the right to exist and develop (Gen. 1; 1 Cor. 15:38-41; Eph. 3:14-15). Thirdly, God's authority is a lawful authority. Though He is above law and not bound by it, as the author of all creation He governs His creatures by law, and promises His covenant faithfulness to that Law-Word. God's Law-Word is refracted within creation into a vast plurality of forms – i.e., for the inorganic and organic world, as well as the total life of man in all his functions and institutions. These laws, norms and ordinances of creation can be studied and understood, and they express the will of God for creation, providing order and constancy and obligating creatures in all their life activities (1 Kings 4:29-34; Ps. 119; Eccl. 1:4-10; Is. 28:23-29). Fourthly and finally, because of God's laws for creation, each person and social institution has the right to exist alongside others with a duty to function in terms of God's Word in creation and Scripture, being obligated to fulfil a specific task and calling in history in terms of God's kingdom (Gen. 1:28; 22:18; Ps. 1; Eccl. 12:13; Matt: 7:26; John 14:21; Rom. 2:6-11):[173]

> The laws of creation, therefore, make possible a plurality of social institutions or spheres, each with a measure of autonomy or sovereignty vis-à-vis all others. The sovereignty of any social sphere, however, is always limited by the sovereignty of co-existing spheres and limited to the task or function to which it is called. Moreover, this earthly sovereignty is subservient to the absolute sovereignty of God. It is delegated by God and remains ever dependent upon Him.[174]

On this view, by virtue of God's creation ordinances and laws for cultural development there are varied differentiated spheres of life within human society including the family, church, state, business, educational institutions, the arts and so forth, which do not *owe their existence* to the state, nor do they *derive their internal sphere of law* from the state. These spheres of life must obey the authority of God and His Word over them. They are not subservient to the state, nor do they relate to the state in *parts-to-whole fashion* as though they were lesser 'parts' of the state. As such the state has no right to overreach and intrude into them. The parts of the state proper are provinces and municipalities, unified under one public legal order within a given territory. Families, churches, schools, businesses etc., may reside and function in that territory, but that does make those entities *parts* of the state.

On this model each sphere is prevented from dominating, controlling and absorbing each other. Instead, each area of life (including the family, church and state) enjoys an internal sovereignty. God has established these various spheres of life to be governed in terms of their own structural principles, ruled by His Word and subject ultimately to Christ as Lord and king. The state does not *grant existence* to the family or the church as though they were lesser parts of itself. Instead, the state must recognize their uniqueness, acknowledge the legitimacy of their relative independence and respect the boundaries of their God-given freedom and authority. This important principle cuts both ways. The church institute does not *grant authority* to the state by directly appointing or anointing it. As Kuyper explains:

> When the state and government are bound to God by a bond *of their own*, even before the church of Christ was there and also without her involvement, then the result is the natural, simplest, and, in comparison with other systems, the most desirable relation of church and state. It is not the church that hands the sceptre to the government…; in the days when Christ was on earth, before his apostles established his churches, Christ himself testified to Pontius Pilate that the power wielded by the Roman emperor and his governor was power given to them by God.[175]

Importantly, this direct accountability of the state to God does not set aside the obligation of churches to preach righteousness in the public space and to prophetically speak truth to power. Nor does it diminish the responsibility of all Christians in *every area of life* and culture to diligently apply their faith and the fulness of the Word of God – whether they are lawyers, politicians, judges, teachers, artists or mechanics. As Kuyper put it, "If one at this point asks whether the Christian religion should not also influence public life, the answer is: without a doubt...; but that influence must come to expression along the constitutional route."[176]

Our secular culture, in the hope of doing away with God's laws and norms for creation, has invariably tried to reduce human social organization and relationships to bare 'natural facts' with merely biological, psychological and economic causal explanations for their existence. But human social relations are not discerned in the same way that we can observe the causal relations in the behavior of a flock of geese – that is, they are not given to us as empirical natural facts. The various typical structures that allow us to distinguish different forms of human social relationship (e.g., family, church and state) are intangible and so the natural sciences cannot discover them. Attempts to 'explain' social structures without creational norms end up explaining nothing. As Dooyeweerd makes clear:

> The state, church, family, marriage, and commercial enterprise, as well as social classes, ranks, and others are not entities that one can weigh and measure. They are not objectively presented to one's sensory perception. One cannot discern or understand them without the application of norms or criteria of propriety. For the very existence of these social relations depends upon these norms, even though in their actual functioning these relations may conflict with such norms. Even the actual activity of a gang of thieves cannot be recognized as such without the application of the norms of an ordered society ... we can never discuss factual social relations in human society without discussing real social norms, even when these relations violate the norms. This also implies it is impossible for sociologists to give a causal explanation without reference to social norms ... if we try to make a consistent attempt to eliminate normative criteria, we shall discover that we end up with no real *human* social facts.[177]

Although the de-Christianizing cultures of the West have sought to shake free from God's revelation in creation and Scripture which delimit the life and institutions of people in terms of normative laws – like logical norms for thought, laws and norms for language, social order, economics, moral and legal life etc., – we find that they are inescapable and cannot be set aside without chaos ensuing. The attempt to be lawless and normless, is entirely self-defeating. The idea of a feeling for justice or a sense of injustice, for example, immediately presupposes normativity. To be human is to be a creature aware of laws and norms that govern our lives in every sphere.

That is obviously not to say that throughout history human beings have positivized (applied and made concrete) God's laws and norms faithfully. Because of sin and rebellion against God, cultural development is shaped by a constant and continual conflict between normative (faithful) and anti-normative (unfaithful) religious motives pulling culture, social structures and relationships in different directions. Just consider today the denial of creational normativity for human identity and sexuality and the consequent efforts to redefine the social and legal structures of marriage and family. In addition, the progress of redemption and historical revelation has opened human eyes in new ways to God's will and purpose so that our understanding is deepened regarding God's law-order. As such, human understanding of the normative role and function of human government has varied and been subject to historical disclosure. Powerful forces driven by deep religious convictions have frequently pushed human society in a totalitarian direction:

> As a religious-political community, the Greek polis [city-state] was totalitarian in nature. It knew nothing of either the modern concept of freedom of certain spheres of life – which as a matter of principle are withdrawn from the state's control – or of the distinction between state and society. Thus, both Plato and

Aristotle treated all sociological questions with the framework of the *politica*, the theory of the polis.[178]

Although a synthesis between the pagan view of the Greco-Roman world and Christianity was attempted in the Holy Roman Empire in the ninth century, biblical faith, especially through the Reformation, provided an alternative view for understanding human society:

> It is the theme of creation, fall into sin, and redemption by Christ Jesus in the communion of the Holy Spirit. It reveals that the religious community of the human race is rooted in creation, in the solidarity of the fall into sin, and in the spiritual kingdom of God through Christ Jesus (the Corpus Christi). In this belief Christianity destroys in principle any claim made by a temporal community to encompass all of human life in a totalitarian sense. It demands internal independence for the church in its relation to the state and sharpens our view of the proper nature of the spheres of life.[179]

The principle of sphere sovereignty thus enables us to distinguish a *just state* from an absolutist *power state*, because a just state will recognize, in terms of the Christian principle, a variety of *spheres of law* within society including *public law, civil private law and non-civil private law*. Public law concerns the constitution, penal law and laws of criminal procedure as well as administrative law, which are meant to guarantee our political freedoms. Common law, or civil private law, exists to guarantee our freedom of thought and expression, association and so forth, making sure that as individuals and social entities we are on an equal footing with others. Critically, non-civil private law concerns the existence and freedom of non-political spheres of law, like the church. Prior to the historical-cultural differentiation of the different spheres of law beginning in the West, with the life of the church institute as independent of the state, undifferentiated societies did not know an independent church, school, or state. Undeveloped societal forms of the extended family, clan, sib and tribe sought to fulfill in an undifferentiated way the tasks and functions of the distinct societal forms we know today. The recognition of distinct spheres of law in Western society is the result of a drawn-out historical process and requires the existence of a genuine state (*res publica*) with an independent and impartial judiciary where decisions are executed by officers of the state. *Public law* is communal law with its own distinct character:

> It comprehends the legal organisation and arrangement of relationships of authority and compliance between government and subjects. This organisation is founded on the sword power of the government and is intended to bring to expression the public legal idea of the common good.[180]

This public law is distinct from the domain of *civil private law* which involves the regulation of private relationships that do not involve authority and subordination. Here the significance and worth of image-bearers as *individuals* is given legal expression regardless of ethnicity, sex, or personal beliefs – it is the asylum of the individual person. Dooyeweerd explains the existence of civil private law:

> It presupposes a high degree of differentiation and integration of legal life and is geared to one structure in human society only, namely that of coordinational civil relationships that fall outside the internal communal and collective spheres of marriage, family, the business firm, organisations, and so on, thus to relationships in which individuals do not exercise any authority over one another ... it presupposes the development of individualized private societal relationships where people participate in coordinated interaction as individual legal subjects with juridical equality. Distinct from the specific private communal law obtaining within particular societal collectivities such as the family, church, school, business, social club, etc., the sole purpose of civil law is to apply the

demands of social justice in the reciprocal private interactions between individuals.[181]

Clearly, none of the jural spheres of human society can exist in isolation. The civil law sphere is obviously intertwined with the state, but it is *not* communal public law. Neither should it be equated with non-civil private law (or private communal law) manifest in the distinct structures of marriage and family, the extended family, the private school, voluntary associations and organizations and the business corporation. Law falling outside the domain of public law is not all private *civil* law, because private law includes various spheres of law which do not have a civil-legal character. Civil private law thus needs to be balanced by the non-civil private law of private communities which should defend their own sphere sovereignty against encroachment by the state:

> What falls outside the domain of civil law is all the specific law of private communities and collectivities which serve their inner structure, guided by a destination lying outside the jural domain. This is the case in internal marriage and family law, internal business law, internal associational law, internal church law, and so on.[182]

This means, for example, that the civil magistrate cannot command or interpret the proper nature of church discipline, doctrine or worship, because this is the domain of non-civil private law and lies outside of the state's competency. It also means that, where civil private law or public law does 'touch' on these non-civil private spheres of authority – say, in the marriage relationship – it does so only with respect to its *external* private civil or public side i.e., the marriage contract/licence and divorce law, or criminal matters in cases of violence or abuse. And the same is true in regard to the church if clergy were assaulting or abusing members. This limitation on the state is necessary because marriage, as an intimate societal form, functions in numerous *internal* relationships like husband and wife, parent and child etc.

Abraham Kuyper explores the institution of the family as a crucial example of a private law sphere which by virtue of its very existence and ordination of God limits the state:

> The sphere of the family opens itself, with its right of marriage, domestic peace, education and possession; and in this sphere also the natural head is conscious of exercising an inherent authority – *not because the government allows it*, but because God has imposed it. Paternal authority roots itself in the very life-blood and is proclaimed in the fifth commandment ... Calvinism protests against state-omnipresence; against the horrible conception that no right exists above and beyond existing laws; and against the pride of absolutism...[183]

This delimiting principle is absolutely vital because most people tend to think of all law as *state law* and all government as *state government*. Yet in terms of the scriptural idea of sphere sovereignty (that is, spheres of law), the state (that is, civil government) is only one form of human government and no state has a legitimate right or authority to invade other law spheres and redefine pre-political societal structures like the family and marriage (let alone biological and creational realities like human sexuality), or to dictate to the church institute how she will worship and govern her members. The same applies to the question of how and what private schools and home schools should teach their children, how a person should decide and conduct their business investments and transactions, or what the artist should paint, or the musician compose and perform. The state only has a valid interest in these matters if and when crimes are being committed or infractions of civil private law come into view. In other words, "Dominion is exercised everywhere," as Kuyper argued, "but it is a dominion which works organically, not by virtue of a state investiture, but from life's sovereignty itself."[184] Thus, the church does not exist by the permission of civil government any more than the family is created by the state. The church is governed and ruled by Jesus Christ under His Word. The state cannot command the church not to preach Christ, baptise or administer the sacraments and exercise church discipline, because Christ Himself and His inspired apostles gave these commands (Matt. 28:16-20; 1 Cor. 11:23-32).

Danie Strauss has pointed out the implications of all this for a Christian view of political life – a just state *must account* for political, communal and personal freedoms. He writes:

> These forms of freedom are correlated with three irreducible jural spheres, namely the sphere of public law, civil private law and non-civil private law. If they are threatened or abolished, we meet a totalitarian and absolutistic state (a power state which is the opposite of a just state), with no guarantees for any form of religious freedom ... the Kingdom message of the New Testament, opens up a dynamic cultural-historical process of differentiation and disclosure in which the state emerges as guided by its sphere-sovereign juridical qualification, alongside a multiplicity of non-political societal entities with their own intrinsic competence to form (non-state) law. When Christians assume responsibility for the unfolding of human societal relationships, the public legal order of the state will not threaten, but protect religious freedom...[185]

It is clear to even the casual observer that Western states today are steadily seeking to abolish the irreducibility of these spheres of law by overreaching into the life of the family, the church institute, the school and business, medicine, private charities and more. This is done primarily by seeking to bring each area of society directly or indirectly under the total control of the state, making them parts or sub-domains of the sphere of public law. Life, sexuality, marriage and historic freedoms are being redefined by unelected judiciaries in the name of Charters and Constitutions (public law), while concurrently, laws are gradually introduced into public criminal or civil codes by an ignorant (and at times malevolent) legislature that undermine personal freedoms historically protected by private civil law, which then also results in the rapid disappearance of the freedoms of the family, church, school and business. In short, the sphere of public law is incrementally eating up the private spheres of law altogether. Increasingly, the citizen stands denuded before the total state, stripped of the protection of mediating non-civil private institutions and even of the inherited liberties of private civil law.

This foreboding totalitarian drift exposes the re-paganization of the Western view of the state – a logical consequence of the de-Christianization of culture. The biblical perspective stands in radical contrast: government expressed in the state is not to be "ruling over the nation for its own profit, but as a God-ordained power to guard the interests of the nation and to honor God in the nation."[186] This implies that each God-ordained sphere of life, created by His Word, is obligated to submit itself to Christ by honoring and respecting each law sphere and keeping within the limits established by God. None of this is to say that the state does not have an important and legitimate role under the sovereignty of God and His Word. But the church, the family, the school and other spheres have their own king, and it isn't the state. As Kuyper puts it in regard to the church institute, "Her position in the state is not assigned her by the permission of the Government, but *Jure divino*. She has her own organisation. She possesses her own office-bearers ... the sovereignty of the State and the sovereignty of the Church exist side by side, and they mutually limit each other."[187]

Ecclesiocracy or Theocracy?

The political implication of sphere sovereignty is thus unequivocally theocratic in the sense that there is no part of the cosmos, no law sphere, no aspect of society or culture that is not being made subject to the Lord Jesus Christ and His Word. The family, the church, the school, the courts, parliament or congress are all called to be expressions, however fallibly, of the *basileia* of God. It is this view of politics alone that protects us from absolutizing and thereby deifying some form of political life. Willem Ouweneel is incisive:

> In socialism, the state is deified; in libertarianism, the individual; in communism the party; and in national socialism, the nation is deified. Only in a truly biblical situation, the state as well as the individual, the party as well as the nation, are directed toward God. We do not serve the state, but the state and we are to serve God ... therefore, every nation state that in principle and in practice, functions out of the acknowledgment of Christ's kingship, also within political life, is a manifestation, no matter how weak, of the kingdom of God.[188]

It is sometimes objected that this kingdom vision of sphere sovereignty under the supreme potentate, Jesus Christ, would *require* some form of establishment – that one church denomination or another must necessarily have its particular confession established and *imposed* if the state is to be genuinely Christian. It is then concluded that to avoid this injustice and potential for persecution of dissenters, we are better off with a secular 'neutral' state pursuing a vague notion of the 'common good' rather than seeking a Christian state that listens to the Word of God.

The neutral state ideal among Christians is influenced by the modernism of both Karl Barth and Emil Brunner. Barth saw the state as a neutral instrument where religious tolerance is the ultimate wisdom[189] and Brunner rejected both abiding creational norms and Holy Scripture as the direct Word of God binding men and nations. The influence of Gnosticism on Brunner in particular is clear.[190] Yet the notion that a Christian state must involve the establishment of a particular church institution is evidently fallacious thinking for several reasons. First of all, as we have already seen, it fails to recognize the true nature of the church in Scripture in its relationship to the *kingdom of God* and continues to think in scholastic terms inherited from pagan Greek thought:

> Paganism, unable to transcend time, seeks a last and highest temporal bond of which all other societal relationships can be no more than dependent parts. *Christianity does not place a temporal church institute above the state as an ultimate bond,* but in Christ it looks beyond time toward the total theocracy, the invisible church of Christ. Here, all temporal societal relationships are rooted and grounded, and each of these, after its own divine structure and God-given law, must be an expression, be it an imperfect one, of that invisible kingdom of God. This basic Christian idea of the kingdom of God is the only possible ground for the Christian idea of the state.[191]

Second, it is inescapable that the state as a societal institution, like all other areas of life, functions in the faith aspect of human experience, making neutrality not just an undesirable but impossible ideal. A democratic state which installs its government through a voting process is run by an elected differentiated public who all bring their *beliefs, convictions and moral commitments* to their work and service. The notion of the 'common good' to be pursued by the state is not self-explanatory and cannot be left as a contentless abstraction, for the question immediately arises, what is the 'good' and how is that to be determined? The reality is that the dominant faith and worldview underlying a culture is a spiritual motive force giving shape to the public life of the state. The naïve idea of a neutral state pursuing a harmony of legal interest in the public square whilst not endorsing both explicitly and implicitly some conception of what is true and good within its laws, constitutional liberties, conception of rights and promotion of justice and fairness, is a mirage. As such, when faithful Christians bring biblical faith to bear in public office, the activity of the state in their orbit would necessarily reflect the impact of Christian principles. When committed secularists and pagans do the same, the state's activity will reflect their principles.

Third, in order for the very concept of Christianity to exist (and therefore the idea of a Christian state), a *mere Christianity* must be definable. There is no reason whatsoever to require that one tradition or sectarian confession be imposed by the state to the exclusion of all the others. All genuinely Christian denominations in the West have for centuries shared in common the ecumenical creeds (Apostles' and Nicene) as a fundamental point of agreement. They have also all regarded (until the invasion of liberalism in the late nineteenth century) the Bible as the Word of God. It is on this ecumenical basis that one could speak of a Christian state led by genuinely Christian faith.

In this regard, it is important to note the difference between *ecclesiastical* confession of faith and *political* confession of faith. The state does not need to 'take a position' on internal ecclesiastical matters such as forms of church government, modes of baptism, confessional tradition, or charismatic gifts. Those are theological developments within various church traditions that are outside of the competency of the state (as a public *legal* order) to address. The church institute is qualified and led by the *faith* aspect (law sphere) of our experience and is concerned with its confession of faith and rites as a believing community. The state is qualified *juridically* and is concerned with the legal order. The Christian state can recognize and affirm in its public communal manifestations (i.e., in its prayers, anthems and constitution) the Lordship of Christ, the foundational creeds of the historic church and the authority of God's Law-Word, without being Baptist, Presbyterian, Roman, or any other denomination. And the legislature can listen (as a legislative body, not as a church body) to the Word of God and the prophetic witness of God's people in faithfully positivizing law in light of Scripture – as the Western tradition has done from the time of King Alfred the Great. In this fashion the state can perform a Christian political integrating function in the faith life of the nation in cultures where the people are marked by a broadly Christian commitment.[192]

Fourth, professing Christian nation states have existed and continue to exist which, however attenuated, have not imposed any particular church's confession. Both Canada and the United States are good examples of historically Christian nations with no federally established church. Even in England where there is now a 'soft establishment,' there has been toleration of all Christian denominations for centuries. Though secularism, humanism and paganism have grown rapidly in North America in the last sixty years and in general the number of committed church-going Christians is in decline, Canada was established as a Christian dominion with a national motto drawn from Psalm 72:8. Even its modern Charter of Rights and Freedoms from 1982 began with a preamble recognizing the supremacy of God. The United States of America, which formally separates church and state (at the Federal level), is possibly the most Christian nation the world has ever known – one nation, under God, as originally conceived. The President still takes his oath of office on the Bible. It used to be taken on a Bible opened at Deuteronomy 27-28, which invokes God's blessing and cursing on a nation for obedience and disobedience. It is therefore demonstrably false to equate the idea of a Christian state or nation with establishment, persecution or the necessity of imposing one church's unique confession on a nation. It was for these reasons, and especially in view of the principle of sphere sovereignty, that Kuyper, over a century ago, lauded the situation in the United States:

> Not a single country can be found in Europe where the relation of state and church is more blessed than in the United States. The national government honors God, does not meddle in ecclesiastical disputes, and is free to set its own course. Conversely, the church of Christ, far from being an obstacle, instead satisfies life's needs with the richest variety, has a place of honor throughout the entire land, is financially independent, and influences public opinion (and through it the president and Congress); it does so to such a degree that no European national church can even begin to be compared with the powerful influence of America's churches on the life of the nation. The churches do not hinder the state in any way, and the state does not place any obstacle in the way of the church's life. Both have complete autonomy and independence.[193]

Naturally, as the United States has seen progressive decline in those confessing the Christian faith, corresponding de-Christianization in culture and growing threats to the freedom of the church politically have developed. The American system was designed for a Christian people, so if the nation continues to wander from the faith, their system of government will continue to steadily come apart.

Nonetheless, Kuyper was right in noting the immeasurable benefits of a free church, in a free nation, that recognizes and honors God. In such a situation no sole church confession is imposed, and godly laws and liberty are among the many fruits of life lived in light of the Word of God. Historically, both Canada and the United States have much to be thankful for in this regard, and much now hangs in the balance. Where a Christian confession among the people is lost, the freedom of the church institute and God's people in every cultural arena will inevitably decline with it. Our era is therefore one of great danger and also of great opportunity. Which one it becomes for the generations that follow very much depends on our level of commitment to the Lordship of Christ today.

The Coercive Character of the State

Throughout this short book I have argued that the principle of *sphere sovereignty*, which is rooted in the Lordship of Christ and authority of His Word, provides the template for organizing a biblical political philosophy, a principle of *resistance* to absolutism, totalitarianism and tyranny. The present cultural situation in the West clearly manifests the urgent need for the recovery of a *distinctly Christian* view of the state in which believers are ready and willing to reckon with the state's inescapably religious character.

The thought of an openly religious state, and the idea of principled resistance to unjust civil authority, will be jarring to the sensibilities of many modern evangelicals. However, I believe this is the clear biblical position. Furthermore, it will not do to say that the perspective I have delineated is just one among many possible and legitimate views of the state available to Christians – allowing us to complacently fall back on the secular liberal status quo and baptise its pagan conceptions as Christian. The principles I have outlined should not be regarded as simply an eccentric or parochial view emerging from Calvinists in the Netherlands and English puritans that we can take or leave depending on our cultural taste and heritage. As Dooyeweerd observed:

> We must protest when other views, which reject this sphere sovereignty because they have compromised with pagan philosophy, are considered as at least comparable Christian views. There is only one Christian view concerning human

relationships which indeed takes seriously, without compromise, the scriptural principle of the kingdom of God.[194]

This point becomes very evident when we notice the consequences of setting the scriptural principle of the kingdom of God aside. If we violate sphere sovereignty and, in secular liberal fashion, bring the properly coercive sword-power of the state into all the organs and institutions of societal life, the character of human society radically changes because the various structures that make up its great diversity are hindered or completely prevented from serving the kingdom of God within their own law sphere. In such a case, the lordship of Christ over them is explicitly or implicitly denied. This problem is magnified tenfold when the state itself loses its moorings in the Christian tradition and instead of maintaining only an *external* and *extensive* relationship to the other spheres of life (touching only their public legal relations and preventing violations of sphere sovereignty), seeks to become *internal* and *intensive* in relation to all the structures of society, reforming them as lesser parts of the state itself.

For example, if a secular liberal civil government runs and funds the sphere of *education* today, you get radical secularization and the imposition of LGBTQ curriculum and neo-Marxist socio-political indoctrination in schools – like it or not. If you bring state power into the pre-political sphere of *family*, you get the redefinition of marriage, bans on discipline and the sexualization and seizure of our children as the state assumes the role of parent – and in some nations like Canada will remove children if state 'therapies' enforcing queer theory are not implemented with confused minors. If you bring government into the sphere of *welfare provision and charity*, you cultivate a radical dependency on an ever-expanding welfare state, undermine the family, promote entitlement and sponsor statist redistribution of wealth in the form of socialism along with the steady collapse of real charity. If you bring the state into the heart of the *church institute,* you get a politicized and regulated church that is unwilling or unable to speak the truth of the gospel and Christ's Lordship to political authorities, and frequently, religious persecution. If you bring the state into the heart of the *economic sphere* with interventionism in free markets, heavy regulation and a burgeoning state bureaucracy employing vast numbers of people, you get socialist collectivism with a 'planned' economy – including minimum wage laws, price fixing and fiat currency with quantitative easing – powerful unions and the steady demise of the free market. If you bring the state into the heart of *medicine* you get medicalized technocratic social planning, coercive state-funded abortion, coercive state-funded euthanasia, state-funded sex change surgery, the denial of the conscience rights of doctors and the indefinite suspension of civil liberties with the mass lockdown of society in the name of *public health* and saving the institutions of socialized medicine (like Britain's National Health Service and Canada's Ontario's Health Insurance Plan). If you bring the civil government into the heart of *media* through state-funded broadcasting and state control you get government media, manipulation of the public narrative, an attack on the free press, various hate speech codes and the attempt to control the dissemination of approved information. All of this control and coercion is inevitable when the state moves beyond its sphere of competency and authority into other sovereign spheres because the state, by its very God-ordained nature, is a *coercive* institution. This is why the state must be delimited by the creational principle of sphere sovereignty. Without this limitation, the state inevitably trends totalitarian, bringing its sword power wherever it goes, in terms of its ideological agenda.

The quasi-religious character of the 'statism' prevalent in the modern West should thus be of profound concern for Christians faced with the all-pervasive dominance of state schools, state-subservient churches, state welfare, state media, state planned economy and state medicine. It forms the creeping basis of a *totalitarian society* and an increasingly absolutist one. The cultural crisis facing believers in recent years has unmasked the extent of our technocratic bureaucratization of life and the disturbing totalitarian drift of a complacent society under the sway of a passive, dependent and docile spirit, ready to run to the state for salvation, safety and provision. Yet there is only one true source of provision and salvation for man and His name is Jesus Christ the Lord. The ever-expanding government of peace is upon His shoulders (Is. 9:6-7) and His dominion is an everlasting dominion (Dan. 4: 34-35).

There is then only one truly Christian view of government and politics that is consistent with the gospel of the kingdom and it involves believers in a critical struggle again in our era. As Evan Runner insightfully articulated it:

> The Christian political task involves calling a halt to the expansionist (totalitarian) politics that emerge in the life of the state where men who do not live by the light of the Word of God and having lost almost all sense of *sphere sovereignty* find themselves with a levelled view of the state and society that knows no limits ordained from above, but only more or less arbitrary limits put by the popular will or the ruler. Here is a problem in the modern world which is overcome by the Christian religion. In the modern political mind, who is there to call the state to order? The meaning of the office in human life has largely been lost; everyman carries the ultimate light around within himself, in his reason, and thus has an equal right with every other to say what the state shall do. Further it has no recognition of divine ordinances. But in the light of scriptural revelation ... who can better call the state to order

than the man who knows himself called to order by the high God? Than the man who trembles before the sovereign Law-Word of God. *The Christian political task is thus concerned with the inner reformation of political life itself as an aspect of the integral renewal of our whole life in obedience to the divine Word of salvation.*[195]

Those who claim allegiance to God in an era of apostasy cannot sit on the fence – we need an undivided heart. We will either be faithful office-bearers calling the state to order in light of the Word of God and His creation ordinances or we will submit ourselves to the arbitrary dictates of the autonomous man and his reason, enabling the ancient idolatry of statism to give shape to the future of our children. Is our ultimate allegiance to the Lord Jesus Christ or to the gods of state like Milcom and Baal in the Older Testament? In his comments on Zephaniah 1, the great nineteenth century English preacher, Charles Spurgeon, points to the divine perspective on those who on the one hand claim to stand with the Most High God, while at the same time bow down to the state as god:

> These people thought they were safe because they were with both parties. They went with the followers of Jehovah and bowed at the same to Milcom. But duplicity is abominable with God, and His soul hates hypocrisy. The idolater who distinctly gives himself to his false god has one sin less than he who brings his polluted and detestable sacrifice into the temple of the Lord, while his heart is with the world and its sins. To hold with the hare and run with the hounds is a coward's policy. In the common matters of daily life, a double-minded man is despised, but in religion he is loathsome to the last degree … how should divine justice spare the sinner who knows the right, approves it, and professes to follow it, and all the while loves the evil and gives it dominion in his heart?[196]

It is surely time for the church with its prophetic voice, and for all God's people in the public sphere, to remind all power and authority that Jesus Christ is Lord and declare with the Psalmist:

> The wicked will return to Sheol—
> *all the nations that forget God.*
> For the oppressed will not always be forgotten;
> the hope of the afflicted will not perish forever.
>
> Rise up, Lord! Do not let man prevail;
> let the nations be judged in Your presence.
> Put terror in them, Lord;
> let the nations know they are only men. (Psalm 9:17-20)

NOTES

1   Jean-Jacques Rousseau, *The Social Contract*, translated by Maurice Cranston (New York: Penguin Books, 1968), 89.

2   George Bernard Shaw, *The Intelligent Woman's Guide to Socialism and Capitalism* (New York: Brentano's Publishers, 1928), 456.

3   "G.B. Shaw 'Praises' Hitler," *New York Times*, March 22, 1935, 21.

4   Paul Johnson, Intellectuals: *From Marx and Tolstoy to Sartre and Chomsky* (New York: Harper, 2007), 243.

5   Johnson, *Intellectuals*, 244 ff.

6   See Roger Scruton, *Fools, Frauds and Firebrands: Thinkers of the New Left* (London: Bloomsbury, 2015).

7   Thomas Sowell, *Intellectuals and Society* (New York: Basic Books, 2011), 4.

8   For a vividly dramatized depiction of this situation, read or watch the play The History Boys by Alan Bennett.

9   D.F.M. Strauss, 'Scholarly Communication,' *Danie Strauss*, http://daniestrauss.com/before2009/DS%202008%20on%20Scholarly%20Communication.pdf, accessed May 6, 2021.

10 Sowell, *Intellectuals and Society,* 93.

11 James Hannan, *The Genesis of Science: How the Christian Middle Ages Launched the Scientific Revolution* (Washington, DC: Regnery Publishing, 2011).

12 H. Evan *Runner, Point, Counter Point* (St. Catharines, ON: Paideia Press, 2020), 43, 45-46.

13 Runner, *Point, Counter Point*, 36.

14 Sowell, *Intellectuals and Society*, 10.

15 Sowell, *Intellectuals and Society*, 94.

16 Stephen D. King, *When the Money Runs Out: The End of Western Affluence* (New Haven, CT: Yale University Press), 120.

17 Johnson, *Intellectuals*, 342.

18 Cited in Johnson, *Intellectuals*, 26–27.

19 Johnson, *Intellectuals*, 25–26.

20 R.J. Rushdoony, *The One and the Many: Studies in the Philosophy of Order and Ultimacy* (Fairfax, VA: Thoburn Press, 1971), 269–71.

21 Julian Huxley, *I Believe: The personal philosophies of twenty-three eminent men and women of our time* (London: George Allen and Unwin, 1944 reprint), 133–134.

22 Thomas Molnar, *Utopia: The Perennial Heresy* (New York: ISI, University Press of America, 1990), 240. I wish to acknowledge my great intellectual debt to, and extensive dependence upon, the incisive analysis of utopian thinking offered in Molnar's book.

23 Huxley, *I Believe*, 111–112.

24 Huxley, *I Believe*, 134.

25 George Orwell, *1984* (New York: Signet 1950 [1949]), 195.

26 J. L. Talmon, cited in Molnar, *Utopia*, 20.

27 Molnar, *Utopia*, 34–35.

28 Egbert Schuurman, *Technology and the Future: A Philosophical Challenge* (Grand Rapids: Paideia, 2009), 345.

29 Edward J. Murphy, "Conflicting Ultimates: Jurisprudence as Religious Controversy," Am. J. Juris. 35 (1990):129.

30 Molnar, *Utopia*, 41–42.

31 Molnar, *Utopia*, 70.

32 Bertrand Russell, *A Fresh Look at Empiricism: 1927–42* (Routledge: London, 1996), 16, cited in Huxley, I Believe, 269–271.

33 For a meticulously researched study of these dramatic changes see, Michael L. Brown, *A Queer Thing Happened to America: And what a Long, Strange Trip it's Been* (Concord, North Carolina: Equal Time Books, 2011).

34 "Bill C-8," Parliament of Canada, accessed July 20, 2021, https://www.parl.ca/DocumentViewer/en/43-1/bill/C-8/first-reading.

35 Andre Schutten, "Federal Liberals Retable Criminal Ban on "Conversion Therapy" with Major Legal Implications for Pastoral Ministry," ARPA Canada, last modified October 1, 2020, https://arpacanada.ca/news/2020/10/01/federal-liberals-retable-criminal-ban-on-conversion-therapy-with-major-legal-implications-for-pastoral-ministry/. Bill C-4 passed into law January 2022.

36 Brown, *A Queer Thing*, 95.

37 Molnar, *Utopia*, 99.

38 Molnar, *Utopia*, 113. Note that in both Marxism and Hitler's National Socialism, the doctrine of evolution in nature played a key role. For Marx, Darwinism justified the class struggle and verified his materialism, for Hitler, evolution justified the elimination of the weak in the creation of the man-god.

39 Julian Huxley, *New Bottles for New Wine* (London: Chatto & Windus, 1959, 1957), 17.

40 James A. Herrick, "C. S. Lewis and the Advent of the Posthuman," John G. West ed. *The Magician's Twin: C. S. Lewis on Science, Scientism, and Society* (Seattle: Discovery Institute Press, 2012), 258.

41 Paul Kurtz (ed.), *Humanist Manifestos I and II* (Buffalo: Prometheus, 1973), 16.

42 Cited by Herrick, C. S. Lewis, 255.

43 Herrick, "C. S. Lewis,"253.

44 Herrick, "C. S. Lewis," 235.

45 Herrick, "C. S. Lewis," 251.

46 Herrick, "C. S. Lewis," 251.

47 Herrick, "C. S. Lewis," 252.

48 *Transcendent Man: The Life and Ideas of Ray Kurzweil.* Directed by Barry Ptolemy, 2009, (Los Angeles, CA: Ptolemaic Productions, 2009), DVD.

49 Herrick, "C. S. Lewis," 252.

50 David Herbert, *Becoming God: Transhumanism and the Quest for Cybernetic Immortality* (Guelph, ON: Joshua Press, 2014), 93.

51 Herrick, "C. S. Lewis," 236.

52 Herrick, "C. S. Lewis," 253.

53 Cited in Herrick, "C. S. Lewis," 237.

54 Herrick, "C. S. Lewis," 256.

55 John Stewart, cited in Herrick, "C. S. Lewis," 251.

56 Herbert, *Becoming God*, 98

57 H. G. Wells, cited in Huxley, *I Believe*, 361.

58 Wells, in *I Believe*, 362.

59 Wells, in *Points of View: A Series of Broadcast Addresses* (London: George Allen and Unwin, 1930), 68. Available online at https://dspace.gipe.ac.in/xmlui/bitstream/handle/10973/22720/GIPE-062996.pdf, accessed February 25, 2022.

60 Wells, in Huxley, *I Believe*, 363.

61 Wells, in Huxley, *I Believe*, 365.

62 Klaus Schwab and Thierry Malleret, *COVID-19: The Great Reset* (Geneva: Forum Publishing, 2020), 78.

63 This happened in early 2013 in Cyprus, when the state directly seized assets from citizen's and foreigner's bank accounts in order to help meet requirements for a banking bailout and preserve their participation in the European Union. See http://www.humanevents.com/2013/04/01/cyprus-meltdown-asset-seizures-to-hit-50-60-or-maybe-even-100-percent, accessed April 16, 2012.

64 See recent policy study commissioned by the Canadian government for imagining Canada's future: canadabeyond150.ca/reports/capital-and-debt.html.

65 Molnar, *Utopia*, 146.

66 R. J. Rushdoony, *The Mythology of Science* (Vallecito, CA: Ross House, 2001), 25–42.

67 Rushdoony, *Mythology of Science*, 43.

[68] Albert Camus, *The Rebel: An Essay on Man in Revolt* (New York: Vintage Books, 1956), 241.

[69] For the highly influential Michel Foucault (perhaps the most cited scholar in the humanities today), the Christian past involves the unjust preservation of an arbitrary worldview that pretends to be true or foundational. In fact, Foucault held, truth or reality is merely a social construct, and past constructs should not bind us in the present. Thus, social reality in our time entangles people in a 'web of oppression.' The oppressor class are the white, male, heterosexual, wealthy, English speaking, able bodied, Christians – outside this group all others are victims of structural oppression to varying degrees. On this view, the personal conduct of an individual is irrelevant to their participation in injustice and oppression. If you share wholly or in part, by birth or by hard work, a good number of the characteristics listed above, you are inescapably a structural oppressor to be judged and cast down to bring about social justice.

[70] Molnar, *Utopia*, 201-202.

[71] Immanuel Kant, *"Perpetual Peace,"* in *Political Writings*, ed. Hans Reiss, trans. H. B. Nisbet (Cambridge, UK: Cambridge University Press, 1970), 105.

[72] Yoram Hazony, *The Virtue of Nationalism* (New York: Basic Books, 2018), 48-50.

[73] Oswald Spengler, *Der Mensch und die Technik*, 45.

[74] Hazony, *The Virtue of Nationalism*, 233-234.

[75] Hazony, *The Virtue of Nationalism*, 53-54.

[76] John Witte, Jr., Introduction, Herman Dooyeweerd, *A Christian Theory of Social Institutions* (La Jolla, CA: The Herman Dooyeweerd Foundation, 1986), 17

[77] Herman Dooyeweerd, *A Christian Theory of Social Institutions* (La Jolla, CA: Herman Dooyeweerd Foundation, 1986), 48.

[78] Augustine, J.G. Pilkington (trans.) *Confessions*. From Nicene and Post-Nicene Fathers, First Series, Vol. 1. Edited by Philip Schaff. (Buffalo, NY: Christian Literature Publishing Co., 1887.) Revised and edited for New Advent by Kevin Knight. http://www.newadvent.org/fathers/110101.htm.

[79] Herman Dooyeweerd, *Roots of Western Culture: Pagan, Secular, and Christian Options*, ed. D.F.M. Strauss (Grand Rapids: Paideia Press, 2012), 92.

[80] Dooyeweerd, *Roots*, 93

[81] His Holiness the Dalai Lama, with Franz Alt, *An Appeal to the World: The Way to Peace in a Time of Division* (New York: HarperCollins, 2017), 4-5.

[82] Danie Strauss, 'The Rise of the Modern (Idea of the) State,' *Politikon*, (August 2006), 33 (2), 183-195.

[83] Dalai Lama, *Appeal*, 10.

84 Friedrich Nietzsche, cited in Kornelis A. Bril, *Vollenhoven's Problem-Historical Method: Introductions and Explorations* (Sioux Center, IA: Dordt College Press, 2005), 97.

85 Bril, *Vollenhoven's Problem-Historical Method*, 93-94.

86 Abraham Kuyper, *Lectures on Calvinism* (Grand Rapids: Eerdmans, 1931).

87 Peter Gay, cited in Bril, *Vollenhoven's Problem-Historical Method*, 95.

88 Charles Taylor, *A Secular Age* (Cambridge, MA: Harvard University Press, 2007), 274.

89 Taylor, *A Secular Age*, 292-293. Emphasis added.

90 Rushdoony, *The One and the Many*, 75.

91 Sartre and Foucault, cited in Bril, *Vollenhoven's Problem-Historical Method*, 97.

92 Francis A. Schaeffer, *The Complete Works of Francis A. Schaeffer, vol. 5: A Christian View of the West* (Wheaton, IL: Crossway, 1982) 375.

93 S. U. Zuidema, *Communication and Confrontation*, (Assen/Kampen: J.H. Kok Ltd, 1972), 154.

94 Schaeffer, *A Christian View of the West*, 378-379.

95 BJ Van Der Walt, *Transforming Power: Challenging Contemporary Secular Society* (Potchefstroom: Institute for Contemporary Christianity in Africa), 207.

96 Schaeffer, *A Christian View of the West*, 381.

97 Van Houten, in Van der Walt, *Transforming Power*.

98 Zuidema, *Communication and Confrontation*, 42, 48-49.

99 Kuyper, *Lectures on Calvinism*, 53-54.

100 Herman Bavinck, *The Certainty of Faith* (St. Catharines, ON: Paideia Press, 1980), 95-96.

101 Duncan Richter, 'Schopenhauer the Optimist,' in *Philosophy Now*, Issue 134, October/November 2019, Anja Publications.

102 For example, Howson's vast piece, 'The Prophecy' (2016) is an absorbing, appalling and devastating depiction of fallen man's condition.

103 Egbert Schuurman, "Creation and Science: Fundamental Questions Concerning Evolutionism and Creationism," in Paul G. Schrotenboer (ed.), *The Reformed Ecumenical Synod*, Vol. VIII, No.2, August 1980.

104 For a helpful explanation of scriptural authority see James R. White, *Scripture Alone: Exploring the Bible's Accuracy, Authority and Authenticity* (Bethany House Publishers: Bloomington, MI: 2004).

105 See R. J. Rushdoony's penetrating study, *The Foundations of Social Order: Studies in the Creeds and Councils of the Early Church* (Vallecito, CA: Ross House Books, 1998).

[106] R.J. Rushdoony, *Roots of Reconstruction* (Vallecito, CA: Ross House Books, 1991), 25.

[107] For Dutch statesman and theologian Abraham Kuyper, the normative operative principle for society under God's sovereignty was called Sphere Sovereignty – a model in which all spheres of power and authority were limited offices to be placed under God's absolute sovereignty.

[108] Strauss, 'The Rise of the Modern (Idea of the) State.'

[109] For an excellent study in the emergence of political freedom in the English-speaking world see Daniel Hannan, *Inventing Freedom: How the English-Speaking Peoples Made the Modern World* (New York: Broadside, 2013).

[110] Helena Rosenblatt, 'A Liberal History,' History Today, Vol 69, Issue 8, August 2019, Walstead Roche, 76-81.

[111] Rosenblatt, 'A Liberal History,' 78.

[112] Cited in Rosenblatt, 'A Liberal History,' 80.

[113] Rosenblatt, 'A Liberal History,' 80-81.

[114] Yoram Hazony, "Conservative Democracy: Liberal Principles have Brought us to a Dead End", *First Things*, January 2019, https://www.firstthings.com/article/2019/01/conservative-democracy.

[115] Hazony, "Conservative Democracy."

[116] Hazony, "Conservative Democracy."

[117] Hazony, "Conservative Democracy."

[118] Samuel Burgess, *The Moral Case for Conservatism* (Exeter, UK: Wilberforce Publications, 2019), 128.

[119] Guillaume Groen Van Prinsterer, *Unbelief and Revolution*, trans. Harry Van Dyke (Bellingham, WA: Lexham Press, 2018), 83.

[120] This point is argued extensively in an excellent new study, Samuel Burgess, *Edmund Burke's Battle with Liberalism: His Christian Philosophy and Why it Matters Today* (Exeter: Wilberforce Publications, 2017).

[121] Burgess, *The Moral Case for Conservatism*, 129.

[122] Burgess, *Edmund Burke*, 43-44.

[123] Cited in Burgess, *Edmund Burke*, 45.

[124] Cf. Gen. 1-2; Is. 24:5-6; John 1:1-13; Acts 17:23-30.

[125] Hazony, "Conservative Democracy."

[126] Burgess, *Edmund Burke*, 52-53.

[127] John Rawls *Political Liberalism* (New York: Columbia University Press, 2005), 463.

[128] Jonah Goldberg, *Liberal Fascism: The Secret History of the American Left, from Mussolini to the Politics of Change* (New York: Broadway Books, 2007), 326-327.

[129] Marcello Pera, *Why We Should Call Ourselves Christians* (New York: Encounter Books, 2008), 33.

[130] Ryszard Legutko, *The Demon in Democracy: Totalitarian Temptations in Free Societies* (New York: Encounter Books, 2016), 65.

[131] See, as a representative sample, Psalm 2; 24; 110; John 1; 1 Cor. 15:24-26; Eph. 1; Phil. 2:9-11; Col. 1; Rev. 1:5.

[132] R.J. Rushdoony, *Christianity and the State* (Vallecito, CA: Ross House Books, 1986), 73-74.

[133] Cf. Prov. 8:15; Is. 40:15-17, 23-24; 49:22-23; John 19:1-11; Rom. 13:1-4; Rev. 1:5.

[134] Cf. Matt. 5:17-20; 24: 35; Acts 7:55-56; Heb. 1:3; 10:12; 1 Cor. 15:24-28; Eph. 1:20-21; Col. 3:1.

[135] Herman Dooyeweerd, *The Struggle for A Christian Politics: Collected Works, Series B – Volume 17* (New York: Paideia Press, 2008), 71.

[136] Abraham Kuyper, Pro Rege: *Living Under Christ's Kingship: Collected Works in Public Theology, Vol 1* (Bellingham WA: Lexham Press, 2016), 72.

[137] Guillaume Groen Van Prinsterer, *Christian Political Action in an Age of Revolution* (Aalten, The Netherlands: WordBridge, 2015), 8, 88-89.

[138] Sean L. Field, "Holy Women and the Rise of Royal Power in France," *History Today*, Vol 69, Issue 10, October 2019, 57.

[139] Abraham Kuyper, *On the Church: Collected Works in Public Theology* (Bellingham, WA: Lexham Press, 2016), 383.

[140] Kuyper, *On the Church*, 387.

[141] According to Bennie van der Walt, no less than 66 popes in the course of history have referred to Thomas Aquinas' philosophy and authority. Aquinas was declared a Saint by the Roman church in 1323 and his thought remains critical to understanding Roman Catholicism as well as a resurgent scholasticism amongst evangelicals.

[142] Kuyper, *On the Church*, 390.

[143] Greg L. Bahnsen, *Theonomy in Christian Ethics* (Nacogdoches, TX: Covenant Media Press, 2002), 505

[144] Kuyper, *On the Church*, 413.

[145] Frank Dikotter, "The Great Dictators," *History Today*, Vol 69, Issue 10, October 2019, 73.

[146] Willem Ouweneel, *The World is Christ's: A Critique of Two Kingdoms Theology* (Toronto: Ezra Press, 2017), 252-254.

[147] Ouweneel, *The World*, 256.

[148] Ouweneel, *The World*, 258.

[149] Ouweneel, *The World*, 261.

[150] Geerhardus Vos, *The Kingdom of God*, (New Jersey: P&R, 1972), 87.

[151] Vos, *The Kingdom of God*, 87.

[152] Vos, *The Kingdom of God*, 77.

[153] Herman N. Ridderbos, *The Coming of the Kingdom* (New Jersey: P&R, 1962), 343.

[154] Ridderbos, *The Coming*, 354-355.

[155] Ridderbos, *The Coming*, 355.

[156] Vos, *The Kingdom of God*, 87-88.

[157] Vos, *The Kingdom of God*, 88.

[158] D.F.M. Strauss, "Sphere Sovereignty, Solidarity and Subsidiarity," *Danie Strauss*, http://daniestrauss.com/selection/DS%202013%20on%20 Sphere%20sovereignty,%20solidarity%20and%20subsidiarity.pdf, accessed October 2019, 99-100.

[159] Herman Dooyeweerd, *The Christian Idea of the State* (New Jersey: The Craig Press, 1968), 12.

[160] Strauss, *Sphere Sovereignty*, 114.

[161] K. L. Grasso, "Dignitatis Humanae," in Weigel & Royal, *A Century of Catholic Social Thought, Essays on Rerum Novarum and Nine Other Key Documents* (Lanham: University Press of America, 1991), 95-113.

[162] Jan Dengerink, *The Idea of Justice in Christian Perspective* (Oshawa: Wedge Publishing, 1978), 3-4.

[163] Dengerink, *The Idea of Justice*, 6.

[164] "The NHS is the world's fifth largest employer," *Nuffield Trust*, last modified October 27, 2017, https://www.nuffieldtrust.org.uk/chart/the-nhs-is-the-world-s-fifth-largest-employer.

[165] See Robert Louis Wilken, *Liberty in the Things of God: The Christian Origins of Religious Freedom* (New Haven: Yale University Press, 2019), 99-117.

[166] Abraham Kuyper, *Christianity as a Life-System: The Witness of a World-View* (Memphis, TN: Christian Studies Centre, 1980), 27.

[167] James M. Willson, *The Establishment and Limits of Civil Government: An Exposition of Romans 13:1-7* (Georgia: American Vision Press, 2009), 14-15.

[168] Willson, *The Establishment*, 26.

[169] Willson, *The Establishment*, 31. Willson's exegetical argument, which cannot be explored here, is worth reading in full.

[170] Kuyper, *Christianity as a Life-System*, 28.

[171] Kuyper, *Christianity as a Life-System*, 28.

[172] Dooyeweerd, *The Christian Idea of the State*, 11.

[173] John Witte, Jr. *Introduction* to Herman Dooyeweerd, *A Christian Theory of Social Institutions* (La Jolla, CA: Herman Dooyeweerd Foundation: 1986), 16-17.

[174] Dooyeweerd, *A Christian Theory of Social Institutions*, 17.

[175] Kuyper, *On the Church*, 414.

[176] Kuyper, *On the Church*, 415.

[177] Dooyeweerd, *A Christian Theory of Social Institutions*, 37-38.

[178] Dooyeweerd, *A Christian Theory of Social Institutions*, 47.

[179] Dooyeweerd, *A Christian Theory of Social Institutions*, 48.

[180] Herman Dooyeweerd, *Time, Law and History: Selected Essays, Collected Works, Series B – Vol. 14*, ed. D.F.M. Strauss (Grand Rapids: Paideia Press), 346.

[181] Dooyeweerd, *Time, Law and History*, 345-346.

[182] Dooyeweerd, *Time, Law and History*, 348.

[183] Kuyper, *Christianity as a Life-System*, 35-36.

[184] Kuyper, *Christianity as a Life-System*, 35.

[185] Danie F.M. Strauss, *Sphere Sovereignty*, (Ezra Institute, March 2019).

[186] Kuyper, *On the Church*, 415.

[187] Kuyper, *Christianity as a Life System*, 38.

[188] Willem Ouweneel, *Power in Service: An Introduction to Christian Political Thought* (St. Catharines: Paideia Press, 2014), 34, 38.

[189] Dengerink, *The Idea of Justice*, 26.

[190] Dengerink, *The Idea of Justice*, 45.

[191] Dooyeweerd, *The Christian Idea of the State*, 10.

[192] Jonathan Chaplin, *Herman Dooyeweerd, Christian Philosopher of State and Civil Society* (Indiana: Notre Dame, 2011), 250.

[193] Kuyper, *On the Church*, 417.

[194] Dooyeweerd, *The Christian Idea of the State*, 11.

[195] H. Evan Runner, *Walking in the Way of the Word: The Collected Writings of H. Evan Runner* (St. Catharines: Paideia Press, 2009), 204-205.

[196] Charles Haddon Spurgeon, *Morning and Evening* (Wheaton: Crossway Books, 2003), daily reader, November 14.